QE2

A 50TH ANNIVERSARY CELEBRATION

CHRIS FRAME AND RACHELLE CROSS

The History Press

For Zac and Callum

Previous page: An Emirates A380-800 makes a low pass over *QE2* as she arrives in Dubai. (Michael Gallagher / Cunard)

Right: Your Guide to QE2 from 1998. (Frame / Cross Collection; reproduced with permission from Cunard)

First published 2017

The History Press
The Mill, Brimscombe Port
Stroud, Gloucestershire, GL5 2QG
www.thehistorypress.co.uk

British Library Cataloguing in Publication Data.
A catalogue record for this book is available from the British Library.

ISBN 978 0 7509 7028 0

Typesetting and origination by The History Press
Printed in India

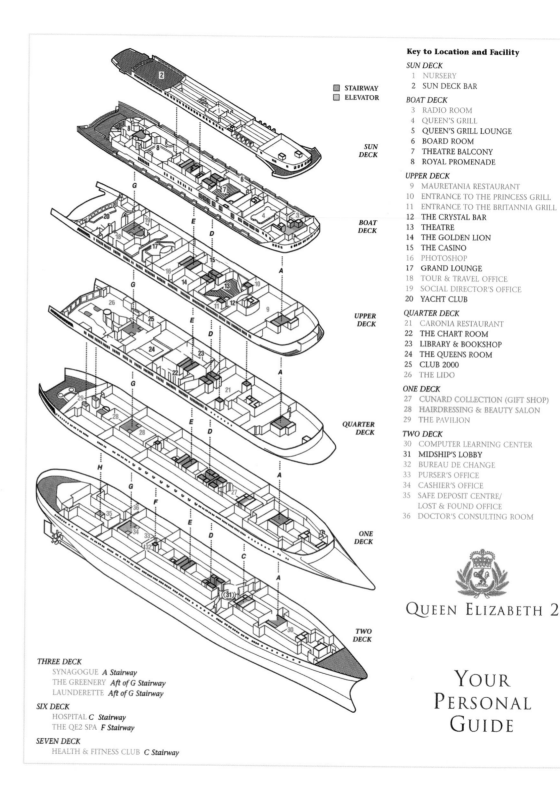

Key to Location and Facility

SUN DECK
1 NURSERY
2 SUN DECK BAR

BOAT DECK
3 RADIO ROOM
4 QUEEN'S GRILL
5 QUEEN'S GRILL LOUNGE
6 BOARD ROOM
7 THEATRE BALCONY
8 ROYAL PROMENADE

UPPER DECK
9 MAURETANIA RESTAURANT
10 ENTRANCE TO THE PRINCESS GRILL
11 ENTRANCE TO THE BRITANNIA GRILL
12 THE CRYSTAL BAR
13 THEATRE
14 THE GOLDEN LION
15 THE CASINO
16 PHOTOSHOP
17 GRAND LOUNGE
18 TOUR & TRAVEL OFFICE
19 SOCIAL DIRECTOR'S OFFICE
20 YACHT CLUB

QUARTER DECK
21 CARONIA RESTAURANT
22 THE CHART ROOM
23 LIBRARY & BOOKSHOP
24 THE QUEENS ROOM
25 CLUB 2000
26 THE LIDO

ONE DECK
27 CUNARD COLLECTION (GIFT SHOP)
28 HAIRDRESSING & BEAUTY SALON
29 THE PAVILION

TWO DECK
30 COMPUTER LEARNING CENTER
31 MIDSHIP'S LOBBY
32 BUREAU DE CHANGE
33 PURSER'S OFFICE
34 CASHIER'S OFFICE
35 SAFE DEPOSIT CENTRE/
   LOST & FOUND OFFICE
36 DOCTOR'S CONSULTING ROOM

STAIRWAY
ELEVATOR

SUN DECK
BOAT DECK
UPPER DECK
QUARTER DECK
ONE DECK
TWO DECK

THREE DECK
   SYNAGOGUE *A Stairway*
   THE GREENERY *Aft of G Stairway*
   LAUNDERETTE *Aft of G Stairway*
SIX DECK
   HOSPITAL *C Stairway*
   THE QE2 SPA *F Stairway*
SEVEN DECK
   HEALTH & FITNESS CLUB *C Stairway*

QUEEN ELIZABETH 2

YOUR
PERSONAL
GUIDE

CONTENTS

(Background image courtesy Jan Frame)

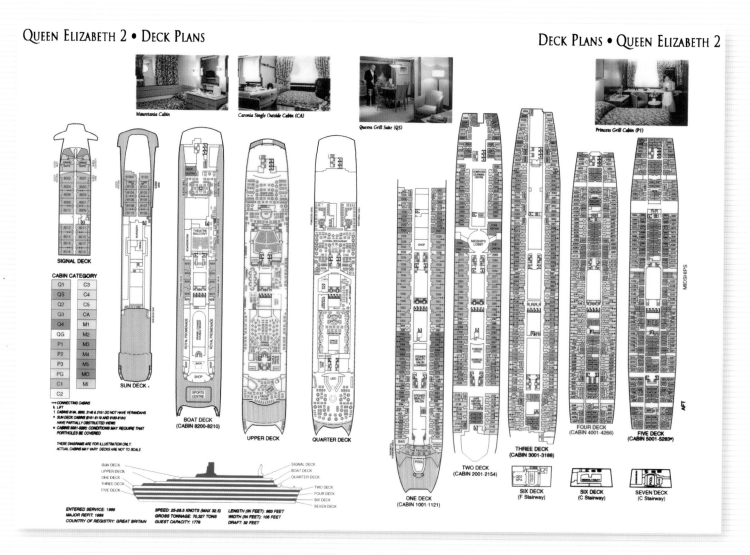

QE2's 1999 deck plans showing the ship's internal layout and imagery of her cabins. (Michael Gallagher / Cunard)

ACKNOWLEDGEMENTS

QE2 is special not only to both of us but also to many people around the world. During her service life she carried 2.5 million passengers and thousands of crew, each of whom played a part in her historic career. We are fortunate that so many of *QE2*'s devotees were available to assist us in writing this 50th anniversary celebration.

Our thanks goes to:

Michael Gallagher, Cunard's official historian, who has supported us in every Cunard book we've written. Michael is a fount of knowledge when it comes to *QE2* and his ongoing assistance, support and fact-checking is very much appreciated.

Captain Ian McNaught, who composed the heartfelt foreword for this book, and provided insights into the magic of *QE2*.

Commodore John Burton-Hall for his poignant afterword to this book as well as information and insights over the past twenty-two years.

Dr Stephen Payne OBE for writing the introduction and providing his unique insight into what made *QE2* special.

Commodore Ronald Warwick for providing photographs, comments and insights into life aboard *QE2* as well as for his ongoing support of our maritime endeavours.

Commodore Christopher Rynd, Captain Chris Wells, Captain Nick Bates, Bill Miller, Carmel Rodgers, Maureen Ryan and Thomas Quinones for their stories and memories.

Rob Lightbody, Lynda Bradford and Isabelle Prondzynski for their stories, memories and remarkable work at The *QE2* Story website and forum. Rob, Lynda and Isabelle, as well as a small group of moderators and over 1,000 members, have posted more than 72,000 stories about *QE2*. The *QE2* Story forum truly does 'keep the legend alive'.

Amy Rigg, Lauren Newby, Glad Stockdale and the whole team at The History Press for their support and passion in making this book a reality.

Alex Lucas, Anders Johannessen, Andy Fitzsimmons, Colin Hargreaves, Gabriele Goldbeck, Ian Boyle (Simplon Postcards), Jan Frame, John and Rosie Burton-Hall, Kenny Campbell, Lloyd Werft Shipyard, Mez Barter, Michael Gallagher, Rob Lightbody, Ronald W. Warwick, Tee Adams, Thad Constantine and Trinity House, for their photographic contributions.

And our families and friends for supporting us.

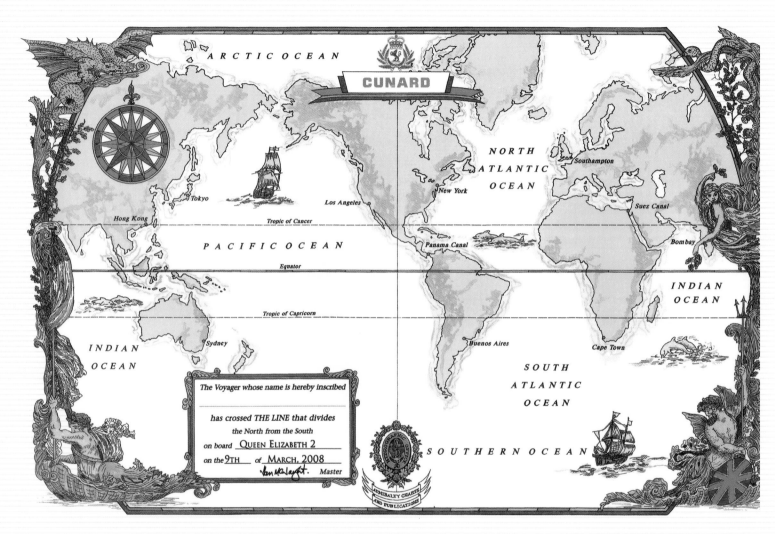

The Voyager whose name is hereby inscribed

————————————————————————

has crossed THE LINE that divides
the North from the South
on board QUEEN ELIZABETH 2
on the 9TH of MARCH, 2008
Master

2008 Final Equator Crossing Certificate. (Frame / Cross Collection;
Reproduced with permission from Cunard)

FOREWORD

BY CAPTAIN IAN McNAUGHT

Fifty years ago, on 20 September 1967, her Majesty the Queen said the words, 'I name this ship *Queen Elizabeth the Second*, God bless her, and all who sail in her.' And so, on that day, on Clydebank, began a most illustrious tale of maritime history – a tale of a great ship fondly known as *QE2*.

For over forty years she sailed the oceans of the world, travelling nearly 6 million miles and carrying 2.5 million passengers. She completed 812 transatlantic crossings, twenty-five world cruises and served her country in the 1982 Falklands campaign.

Her days ended on 27 November 2008 when, at 2.05 p.m. local time in Dubai, I, as her final master, made the closing entry in the logbook and then attended the handing-over ceremony on the Bridge wing. The Cunard house flag, paying off pennant and Red Ensign were lowered and the ship was handed over to her new owners, Nakheel Dubai.

As I write, she looks somewhat forlorn at her berth in Dubai. Her lifeboats and davits have been removed, the Cunard lettering under the Bridge wings has gone and it no longer says 'Southampton' on the stern.

I hope she has a happy ending, unlike her predecessor *Queen Elizabeth* in Hong Kong, and that in ten years' time we can celebrate the sixtieth birthday of what I always thought was 'the greatest ship in the world'. Whatever happens to her, I know we shall never see the like of her again, and I hope this book will bring back happy memories of a much loved and cherished ship, the crew who gave her heart and made it all work, and the passengers who sailed with us.

Top left: Captain Ian McNaught in his office aboard *QE2*, 2008. (Frame / Cross)

Top right: *QE2* being manoeuvred by a Sydney Harbour tug during her final Australian visit in 2008. (Frame / Cross)

Above: *QE2* made several maiden calls during her final season. One such call was at Albany, Australia, on 4 March 2008. (Frame / Cross)

Right: *QE2* at sea as pictured from her starboard Bridge wing. (Frame / Cross)

INTRODUCTION

BY DR STEPHEN PAYNE OBE

I remember, as a young boy of 7, watching the spectacle of a great ship being launched: the graceful hull moving slowly at first down the slipway, before increasing momentum led to a thundering charge that was only finally arrested by a mass of heaving drag chains immediately the ship entered the water. The ship was Cunard's new superliner: *Queen Elizabeth 2*, or *QE2* as she became popularly known. I could never have imagined then that thirty years later I would lead the team designing and producing the ship that would ultimately replace *QE2* and keep Cunard's transatlantic legacy alive, namely *Queen Mary 2*.

QE2 as seen during her sea trials. Her terraced aft decks and twin swimming pools made her well suited for cruising. (Michael Gallagher / Cunard)

Throughout my early life, *QE2* featured prominently as an icon of passenger ships. She was at that time one of only a handful of what I call 'true liners' left, forged in the same mould as *Canberra*, *France* and *Rotterdam*. By the time I came to work on *Queen Mary 2* she was the last.

Queen Elizabeth 2 never had it easy. She was created as a dual-purpose vehicle from the debacle of an earlier plan to build a single-purpose transatlantic liner. She was radically different, internally and externally – so much so that Cunard purists initially hated her.

She was born to an organisation that was struggling to find its place in the modern post-jet world, which would ultimately soon succumb to a successful takeover bid from a company that hitherto had never had a leisure-focused component. This in turn would lead to a drastic reappraisal of *QE2* and a radical reorganisation of the ship and the way in which she was operated. It is almost certain that without these changes Cunard and *QE2* would never have weathered the consequences of the fuel crisis of the early 1970s. However, the resulting intensification of her service commitments led to serious reliability issues due to the absence of a fourth boiler that would have provided better maintenance possibilities – removed from plans as a cost-cutting measure during her construction. Re-engining from steam to diesel-electric solved many of these issues, whilst a major midlife refit of

QE2's original forward profile. Large windows wrapped around Upper Deck allowed a forward view for passengers. (Michael Gallagher / Cunard)

QE2 was registered in Southampton from 1969 to 2008. (Frame / Cross)

the passenger spaces would transform for the first time the rather piecemeal in-service adaptations of her interiors into a co-ordinated ensemble.

QE2 endured all of these trials and tribulations, and sailed serenely on in peace and war as one of the world's favourite ships, becoming ultimately part of Carnival Corporation's sprawling empire. She was finally sold with the promise of a golden future as part of a sun-kissed resort; these aspirations haven't been fulfilled. *QE2* lingers on in moribund isolation, her final chapter yet to be written.

In *QE2: A 50th Anniversary Celebration*, Chris Frame and Rachelle Cross keep the glorious memories alive and herald the achievement of the ship, her designers and builders. It is a commemoration story that deserves to be told, as much of the modern-day cruise industry is based on the legacy of *QE2*.

QE2 at anchor off Zakynthos during her 2008 'Mediterranean Sojourn' voyage. (Frame / Cross)

KEY *QE2* SPECIFICATIONS

GENERAL INFORMATION (DURING CUNARD SERVICE)

Gross Registered Tonnage (1969): 65,862 tons.

Gross Registered Tonnage (2008): 70,327 tons.

Length: 963ft.

Width: 105.25ft.

Builders: John Brown Shipyard / Upper Clyde Shipbuilders.

Keel Laid: 5 July 1965.

Launched: 20 September 1967 by HM Queen Elizabeth II.

Maiden Voyage Departure: 2 May 1969.

Final Day of Service: 27 November 2008.

Maximum Passenger Capacity (2008): 1,777 persons.

Standard Crew Capacity: 1,040 persons.

Port of Registry (1969–2008): Southampton, England.

Official Number: 336703.

Official Signal Letters: G.B.T.T.

THE ENGINES AND MACHINERY ABOARD *QE2*

ENGINE INFORMATION (1967–86)

Engines: 2 x double reduction geared turbines.

Boilers: 3 x high-pressure water tube boilers, 278 tons each.

Propellers: 2 x six-bladed fixed-pitch propellers.

Output at Propellers: 110,000 shaft h.p.

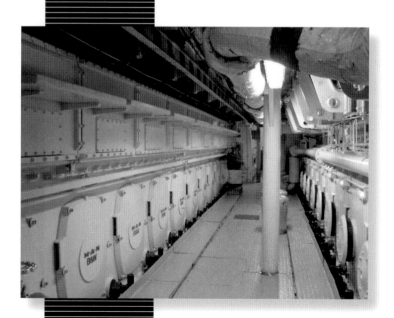

Lower level of the diesel engine room, between two of the nine engines. (Frame / Cross)

The upper level of one of *QE2*'s two diesel engine rooms. (Frame / Cross)

ENGINE AND MECHANICAL INFORMATION (1987–2008)

Diesel Engines: 9 x nine-cylinder MAN B&W diesels.

Electric Motors: 2 x 350-ton, one on each propeller shaft.

Boilers: 9x exhaust gas. 2 x oil-fired.

Propellers: 2 x five-bladed outward-turning LIPS controllable pitch propellers.

Output at Propellers: 44MW each.

Fuel Consumption: 18.05 tons per hour (433 tons per day) on nine diesels.

The engine control room as it appeared from 1987. (Frame / Cross)

OTHER MECHANICAL INFORMATION (AS AT 2008)

Bow Thrusters: 2 x Stone Kamewa, 1000h.p. each.

Stabilisers: 4 x Denny Brown.

Rudder Weight: 75 tons.

Forward Anchors: 2 x 12½-ton.

Forward Anchor Cables: 2 x 1,080ft-long.

Aft Anchor: 1 x 7¼ tons.

Aft Anchor Cables: 1 x 720ft-long.

Service Speed: 28.5 knots.

Top Cruising Speed: 32.5 knots.

1964

9 September	Tenders to build Q4 are called for.
30 November	Cunard receives all viable bids for Q4.
30 December	Sir John Brocklebank of Cunard and Lord Aberconway of John Brown sign a contract to build Q4. She is job No. 736.

1965

5 July	736's keel is laid.

1967

20 September	The ship is launched by HM Queen Elizabeth II who names the ship *Queen Elizabeth the Second*.

1968

19 November	Prince Charles sails aboard *QE2* as her first official 'passenger'.
26 November	*QE2* begins her preliminary sea trials.
30 November	Fuel oil contaminates *QE2*'s steam propulsion system during trials. She returns to Greenock for repairs.
18 December	*QE2* begins her second technical trials.
23 December	*QE2* begins her acceptance sea trials.
24–28 December	*QE2*'s engines malfunction during trials, delaying her acceptance.

1969

25 March	*QE2* begins her belated builders technical trials.
27 March	*QE2*'s sea trials are finally successfully completed.
30 March	*QE2* commences a shakedown cruise.
18 April	Cunard take possession of *QE2*. She becomes the Cunard flagship.
22 April	*QE2* begins her trial 'mini maiden voyage'.
30 April	*QE2* returns to Southampton after her 'mini maiden voyage'.

1 May	HM Queen Elizabeth II and HRH the Duke of Edinburgh tour the completed *QE2*.
2 May	*QE2* departs Southampton on her maiden voyage.
7 May	*QE2*'s maiden arrival in New York.

1971

| 8 January | *QE2* goes to the aid of the stricken French Liner *Antilles*. |
| 26 August | Trafalgar House Co. acquires Cunard. |

1972

| 17–18 May | A bomb threat is received by *QE2*. Bomb-disposal team is parachuted into the sea and retrieved by *QE2*'s crew. No bomb is found. |
| October | The first block of balcony suites is added to *QE2* in Southampton. |

1975

| 10 January | *QE2* sets sail on her first world cruise. |
| 25 March | *QE2* transits the Panama Canal for the first time, making her the largest liner to transit the canal at the time (taking the record from the 1929-built German liner *Bremen*). |

1977

| 3 December | *QE2* begins refurbishment in New Jersey. Here the Queen Elizabeth and Queen Mary suites are added to the ship's Signal Deck. |

1982

| 3 May | *QE2* is called into military service for use as a troop carrier in the Falklands campaign. |
| 4 May | *QE2* arrives in Southampton and is registered as Ship Taken Up From Trade (STUFT). |

12 May	3,000 troops board *QE2* for the journey south.
27 May	*QE2* arrives in Cumberland Bay, South Georgia.
28 May	The troop transfer from *QE2* to *Canberra* commences.
11 June	*QE2* arrives back in Southampton. HM the Queen Mother sails out aboard the Royal Yacht *Britannia* to welcome the troops home.
12 June	*QE2* begins her post-war refurbishment.
15 August	*QE2* returns to passenger service. She wears a light pebble-grey livery and Cunard colours on her funnel.

1986

| 20 October | *QE2* embarks on the last Cunard transatlantic steam crossing. This marks the end of Cunard's regular steam-powered transatlantic crossings, which had run from July 1840 to October 1986. |
| 27 October | *QE2* arrives in Bremerhaven, Germany, for conversion to a diesel-powered ship. |

1987

20 February	The ship's distinctive new wider funnel is lowered aboard.
25 April	*QE2* is returned to the Cunard Line.
28 April	*QE2* arrives in Southampton for the first time under diesel power.
29 April	HRH Princess Diana visits *QE2* with a group of schoolchildren. *QE2* departs on her first transatlantic crossing under diesel power.

1988

| 23 July | New five-bladed propellers are fitted to *QE2* in Bremerhaven. |

1989

| 27 March | *QE2* is chartered for seventy-two days in celebration of the 130th anniversary of Yokohama. |

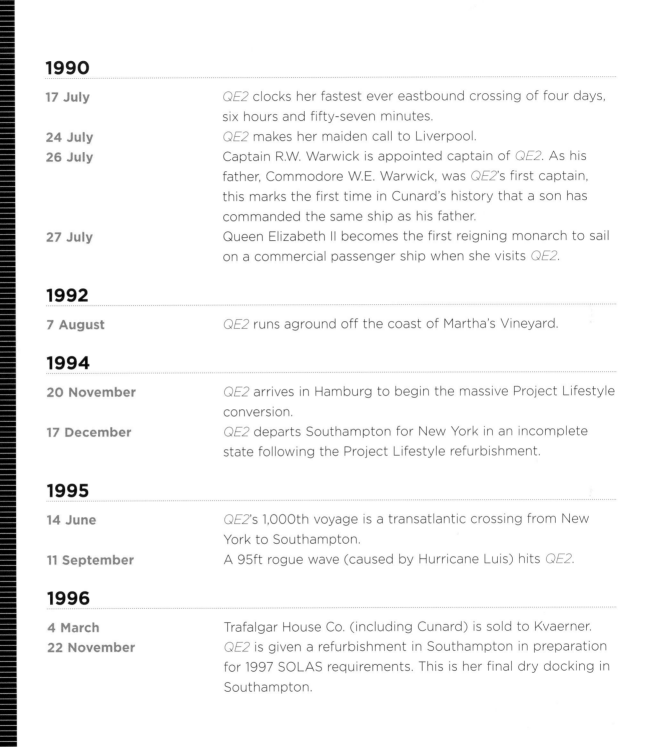

1990

17 July	*QE2* clocks her fastest ever eastbound crossing of four days, six hours and fifty-seven minutes.
24 July	*QE2* makes her maiden call to Liverpool.
26 July	Captain R.W. Warwick is appointed captain of *QE2*. As his father, Commodore W.E. Warwick, was *QE2*'s first captain, this marks the first time in Cunard's history that a son has commanded the same ship as his father.
27 July	Queen Elizabeth II becomes the first reigning monarch to sail on a commercial passenger ship when she visits *QE2*.

1992

7 August	*QE2* runs aground off the coast of Martha's Vineyard.

1994

20 November	*QE2* arrives in Hamburg to begin the massive Project Lifestyle conversion.
17 December	*QE2* departs Southampton for New York in an incomplete state following the Project Lifestyle refurbishment.

1995

14 June	*QE2*'s 1,000th voyage is a transatlantic crossing from New York to Southampton.
11 September	A 95ft rogue wave (caused by Hurricane Luis) hits *QE2*.

1996

4 March	Trafalgar House Co. (including Cunard) is sold to Kvaerner.
22 November	*QE2* is given a refurbishment in Southampton in preparation for 1997 SOLAS requirements. This is her final dry docking in Southampton.

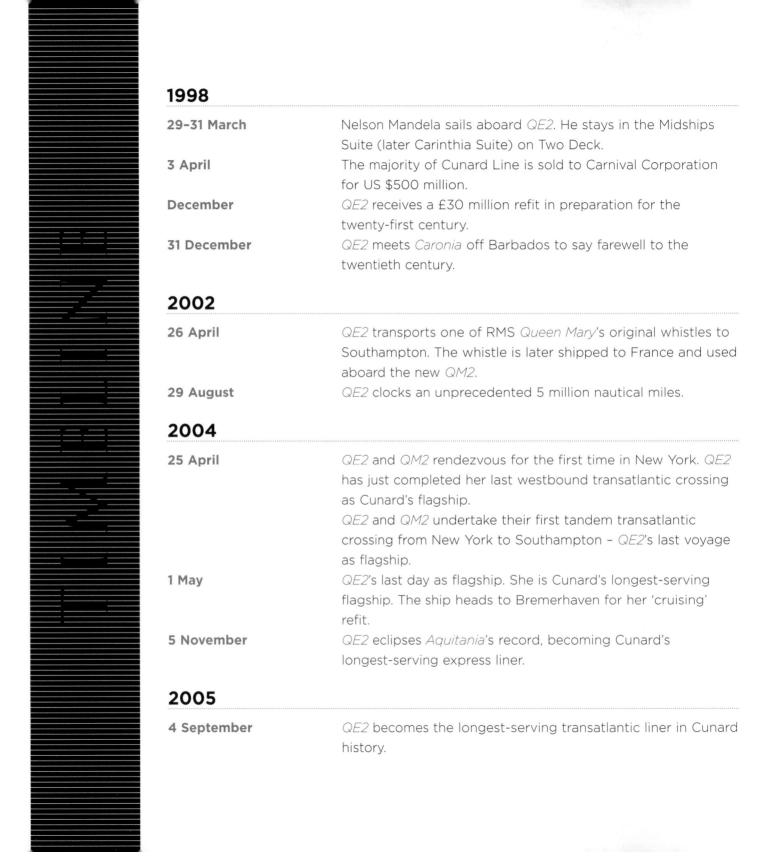

1998

29–31 March Nelson Mandela sails aboard *QE2*. He stays in the Midships Suite (later Carinthia Suite) on Two Deck.

3 April The majority of Cunard Line is sold to Carnival Corporation for US $500 million.

December *QE2* receives a £30 million refit in preparation for the twenty-first century.

31 December *QE2* meets *Caronia* off Barbados to say farewell to the twentieth century.

2002

26 April *QE2* transports one of RMS *Queen Mary*'s original whistles to Southampton. The whistle is later shipped to France and used aboard the new *QM2*.

29 August *QE2* clocks an unprecedented 5 million nautical miles.

2004

25 April *QE2* and *QM2* rendezvous for the first time in New York. *QE2* has just completed her last westbound transatlantic crossing as Cunard's flagship.

QE2 and *QM2* undertake their first tandem transatlantic crossing from New York to Southampton – *QE2*'s last voyage as flagship.

1 May *QE2*'s last day as flagship. She is Cunard's longest-serving flagship. The ship heads to Bremerhaven for her 'cruising' refit.

5 November *QE2* eclipses *Aquitania*'s record, becoming Cunard's longest-serving express liner.

2005

4 September *QE2* becomes the longest-serving transatlantic liner in Cunard history.

2006

24 April — *QE2* commences a sixteen-day refurbishment at Lloyd Werft, Bremerhaven.

2007

18 June — *QE2*'s retirement is announced while the ship is on a cruise to Norway.

20 September — It is forty years since *QE2*'s launch. She returns to the River Clyde to mark the occasion.

2008

11 November — *QE2* runs around on her final Southampton arrival. That night, she departs Southampton for the last time.

26 November — *QE2*'s arrival in Dubai is marked by an A380 flyover and an escort in the form of Royal Yacht *Dubai* and HMS *Lancaster*.

27 November — The last passengers disembark. The Cunard flag is lowered for the last time as *QE2* is handed over to her new owners.

2009

July — *QE2* is moved to the Dubai dry dock and inspected, painted, cleaned and prepared for what is expected to be a long voyage to South Africa for use as a floating hotel for the FIFA World Cup.

2011–12

31 December –1 January — The New Year's Eve party aboard *QE2* is the first and only public event aboard the ship since she arrived in Dubai.

2013

17 January — The plans for Hotel QE2 Asia are announced and *QE2* is relocated to the Dubai dry dock.

2015

August   *QE2* is relocated back to Port Rashid and cleaned over
several days.

2016

August   *QE2*'s lifeboat davits are cut from the ship, the first major
alteration to her exterior profile.

2017

20 September   *QE2*'s 50th anniversary is celebrated aboard MV *Queen
Elizabeth*, as well as at Clydebank where the ship was built.
QE2 remains at Port Rashid in Dubai.

one

THE WORLD'S BEST-LOVED SHIP

I name this ship *Queen Elizabeth the Second*.

HM the Queen at *QE2*'s launch

There are few names in the annals of transportation history that evoke a sense of luxury, heritage and timelessness the way that *QE2* does. Launched on 20 September 1967 by HM the Queen, *QE2* went on to have a thirty-nine-and-a-half-year service career, longer than any large express liner before her.

QE2 is quite possibly the world's most beloved ship. She carried more passengers than any ship has done in the long history of ocean travel. *QE2* travelled over 5.6 million miles during her career with Cunard, making her the furthest-travelled ship ever. Throughout her service life, *QE2* was the Queen of the Seas. She was a British ambassador, a floating icon, and she attracted attention like a worldwide celebrity.

Even today, after having been laid up for the better part of a decade, *QE2* is fondly remembered by people across the globe. If you check social media, her name is often mistakenly used when people spot *Queen Mary 2* or the new *Queen Elizabeth* in ports across the world. In fact, the name *QE2* is practically interchangeable with 'luxury cruise ship' – it is a household name.

So why was *QE2* so popular? What made her so successful? There is no simple answer to these questions other than to say that, above all else, *QE2* was the ultimate example of the end product being more than the sum of its parts. The ship was more than the aluminium and steel that made her up. She was dynamic, vibrant and full of life.

QE2 was built at a time when ocean liners were being retired en masse. She was to be the last Cunard-commissioned ocean liner, and was the final express liner built in Great Britain. *QE2* was the final Cunard contract at the John Brown Shipyard, the last transatlantic liner built in Scotland and the last transatlantic liner designed in the Cunard Building in Liverpool. Before she even entered the water, this made *QE2* famous, iconic and important.

Her early months were fraught with problems. Funding issues, looting epidemics, broken engines and Cunard's refusal to accept delivery of the unfinished ship all threatened to undermine the reign of this final British Queen. But thanks to *QE2*'s first devotees – those at Cunard and the shipyard – she was finally delivered in 1969 and became an international hit. Her classic 1960s interior and sleek, speedy exterior made her radically different from the ageing Cunard fleet of the early part of that decade. A whole new breed of traveller started to sail aboard *QE2*.

As her regular travellers matured, so did the ship. It's hard to pinpoint any other major express liner that had as many alterations, facelifts and refurbishments as *QE2*. But that

Left: The original stylised logo for *QE2*. Its design, which depicts the letters Q, E and the number 2 in a single emblem, was found on brochures, deck plans and aboard the ship. (Michael Gallagher / Cunard)

Below: Members of *QE2*'s first crew take in the view from Two Deck. (Michael Gallagher / Cunard)

THE CREW

CAPTAIN MCNAUGHT
QE2'S FINAL MASTER

~~~

Memories of QE2? There is so much to recall it is almost impossible to pick one single event or person. Being there as her last master was very special; meeting HM The Queen, HRH Prince Philip, Baroness Thatcher or David Bowie, and a whole host of other well-known people was always a great honour; but for me the special memories will always be of the ship's company over all my years there. It is they who gave the ship her soul. It is they who set the tone and atmosphere on board and gave the ship her character.

I think QE2 was special. There were a few who served on the ship throughout her life, there were many who stayed on her for many a year, and I know our passengers had a special relationship with us. The bedroom steward, the waiter, the barman were among the people who made our passengers feel special, but there were many behind the scenes as well, the sailors, the engineers, plumbers, laundrymen, pot washers, to name a few, who rarely or even never in some cases came into contact with passengers, but without whom the ship could never run. It took all 1,020 of us to make the magic happen.

A captain is only as good as his crew, so on behalf of me, and the passengers, may I say thank you to all who served on QE2 for making her so special over so many years.

The ship at sea prior to the 1994 refit. The two large tenders 'Alpha' and 'Beta' were removed during that refit. (Michael Gallagher / Cunard)

Left: *QE2* at sea makes for an impressive sight. Here you can see the glass 'magrodome' roof atop *QE2*'s Quarter Deck swimming pool. (Michael Gallagher / Cunard)

Above: *QE2* departs Fremantle, Australia in 2008. This was her final call to an Australian port. (Alex Lucas)

FROM LAUNCH TO RETIREMENT

LYNDA BRADFORD

MODERATOR AT THE *QE2* STORY FORUM

My first memory of *QE2* was the construction of the ship in Clydebank and the excitement in the town in the build-up to her launch, on 20 September 1967. I was working that day, but I heard the salute given by ships and shipyards on the River Clyde when she was launched. It was at that moment I first knew she was special. When I went home, I said to my father, 'What an amazing reception for the new ship.' My father's response was that she was no ordinary ship: she was a Queen! My dad, who was a managing foreman at John Brown Shipyard, asked me if I would like to go into the yard at the weekend to see her. As a result of the invite, I stood on the decks of *QE2* just days after she was launched, and this was the start of my love for the ship.

In November 1968, friends and family of John Brown's employees had the opportunity to see around *QE2* before she left Clydebank. I was lucky to get a ticket, to view the ship on 15 November, between 6.45 p.m. and 7.30 p.m. I can remember the excitement of going through the shipyard gates and seeing her there, looking magnificent. The glow of the interior lights made the ship stand out against the night sky. Once on board, I followed the procession of people viewing the luxury cabins and the elegant public rooms. I remember being most impressed with the modern curved glass and aluminum staircase, linking the Double Up Double Down room. The memory of approaching from Boat Deck on the upper level and gliding down the stairs remains with me to this day.

Almost thirty years later, in 1997, I sailed for the first time as a passenger on *QE2*. There had been many changes to the interior design that gave a timeless elegance to the ship. Public rooms, restaurants and bars had been remodelled, but as I explored, I could still visualise *QE2*, built and fitted out in Clydebank, that I had viewed in 1968. Words cannot describe my emotions as I stepped aboard and into the Midships Lobby, to the sound of the harpist playing. It was like a dream come true!

Today I am a moderator on The *QE2* Story Internet forum, helping to keep the memory of *QE2* alive – all for the love of a very special ship!

QE2 in Sydney surrounded by tugboats, which were required to assist the ship when manoeuvring. (Frame / Cross)

seemingly constant change allowed the ship to evolve from a 1960s-style floating resort, to a classic stately home at sea, just as the guests who were in their 20s when she entered service were themselves ageing and maturing.

Circumstance also added to the mystique of *QE2*. Her early encounters with danger in the way of rescue missions, pioneering voyages to Israel and bomb scares put her in the headlines. And in the 1980s, her service for Queen and country during the Falklands War was the keystone in her becoming the immortal flagship of Great Britain.

Throughout each chapter of her career, the constant professionalism, passion and dedication of the captains, officers and the countless crew who served aboard her gave returning passengers a sense of family, while newcomers were whisked away into another world, where time felt like it slowed. When *QE2* retired from service in 2008, there were still members of the ship's company who had crewed the ship during her maiden voyage – a remarkable feat in the fast-paced, quick-turnover world of modern employment.

This book was created to celebrate the 50th anniversary of *QE2*'s launch – the day the legendary liner was named *Queen Elizabeth 2*.

two

SETTING THE STAGE

Flying is a fad.

Unnamed Cunard director when faced with the prospect of jet
services eclipsing transatlantic ocean liner travel

QE2's origins can be traced back to 1839, when Canadian-born Samuel Cunard won the British Government's transatlantic Royal Mail contract. His success at securing the mail contract led to the formation of the British and North American Royal Mail Steam Packet Co., which quickly became known as 'Cunard's Line'. A fleet of four paddle steamers, *Britannia*, *Acadia*, *Caledonia* and *Columbia*, each of them around 200ft long, allowed Cunard to establish the world's first regular scheduled transatlantic steamship mail and passenger service. The first voyage was aboard *Britannia* in 1840. It was a resounding success, and the stage was set for the evolution of transatlantic liners that would lead to the construction of *QE2*.

Over the years, transatlantic liners became key pieces of infrastructure in a rapidly changing world. They were instrumental in the building of nations, technological progress and the mass transportation of goods. Competition between lines from Britain, Germany, France, Italy and the United States saw shipping designs balloon into gigantic vessels the likes of which Samuel Cunard could have only dreamed of. By the early twentieth century, liners had eclipsed 30,000 tons. Immigration from Europe to America was the main driving force behind the growth of liners; millions of people relocated in the early 1900s. This boom in immigration led Cunard to build some of the finest ships of their day: *Lusitania*, *Mauretania* and *Aquitania*.

Fifteen years later, during the inter-war period, plans were well under way for the first of a new breed of Cunarder: the *Queen Mary*. *Queen Mary*'s design eclipsed 80,000 tons, making her significantly larger than the Cunard ships she replaced.

From 1921, the American Government began considerably reducing immigration quotas. Thus, commerce and tourism became the new driving force in the growth of passenger ships in the late 1920s and early 1930s. A new class of passenger, the American traveller, filled the tourist-class berths on eastbound crossings, eager to explore Europe and beyond.

Queen Mary was not alone. Her main rival was the equally large and even more opulent French liner *Normandie*. But the then Cunard–White Star had an ace up its sleeve: a fleet mate for *Queen Mary*. Named *Queen Elizabeth*, she was the largest passenger ship ever built – a title she held until 1996, when *Carnival Destiny* finally eclipsed her in size.

The Queens allowed Cunard to achieve its long-held ambition of a two-ship weekly transatlantic service, which it established after the Second World War. The liners' immense size, coupled with top speeds in excess of 28 knots, gave them the edge over their rivals, with both ships enjoying great popularity. Celebrities, dignitaries, politicians and, importantly, the average citizen flocked to the Cunarders to experience a fast ocean crossing, in which 'getting there was half the fun'.

Above: Sir Samuel Cunard formed the Cunard Line. He was depicted in *QE2*'s Midships Lobby. This mural, one of four by Peter Sutton, formed the starting point of the Cunard Heritage Trail. (Frame / Cross)

Left: *Mauretania* entered service in 1907 and captured the transatlantic speed record. She held the accolade until 1929. (Ian Boyle / Simplon Postcards)

Mauretania featured in *QE2*'s Midships Lobby. Here she is depicted in a mural by Peter Sutton, alongside imagery of traditional shipboard entertainment. (Frame / Cross)

Above left: *Queen Mary*'s shopping promenade was completed in an art deco style. (Ian Boyle / Simplon Postcards)

Above: *Queen Elizabeth* began her career as a troopship in the Second World War, only entering Cunard passenger service after the conflict ended. (Ian Boyle / Simplon Postcards)

Left: *Queen Elizabeth* and her fleet mate *Queen Mary* were the first express liners to successfully establish a two-ship weekly transatlantic service. (Ian Boyle / Simplon Postcards)

As the jet airliner became more popular, Cunard sent *Queen Elizabeth* cruising. (Ian Boyle / Simplon Postcards)

Queen Mary docked at the old Ocean Terminal in Southampton. This dock was rebuilt into the Queen Elizabeth II Terminal, which *QE2* often frequented. (Colin Hargreaves)

The Three Graces in Liverpool. The square building in the centre is the Cunard Building where *QE2* was designed. (Mez Barter)

Caronia was designed as a 'dual-purpose liner' allowing her to cruise as well as complete transatlantic crossings. (Ian Boyle / Simplon Postcards)

The Queens' main rival in the post-war years was the American liner *United States*. Though smaller than the Cunarders, *United States* was still a large ship at 990ft and 53,330 gross tons. When she entered service in 1952, her sleek lines and gigantic funnels, painted proudly in red, white and blue, made her stand out among the more traditional liners plying the Atlantic. But the true appeal of *United States* was her speed. She easily outpaced the Queens and captured the transatlantic speed record for America on consecutive east- and westbound crossings. She remains to this day the fastest passenger liner ever to set sail.

However, as the 1950s drew to a close, a new, unbeatable threat entered the transatlantic arena: the jet airliner. First the Comet 4, then the far more successful Boeing 707 and Douglas DC-8, completely revolutionised international travel. Jet aircraft services meant the transatlantic journey could now be completed in just a few hours – why would anyone spend up to a week on a ship? Cunard at first believed the answer was the timeless elegance of the Queens. In fact, one director is noted as saying 'flying is a fad.' The reality, however, was that most people chose to fly. Within a decade, transatlantic passenger shipping had collapsed. Cunard retired its giant Queens, along with the vast majority of its fleet.

three

A GREAT GAMBLE

This confirms our intention to stay in the forefront of the North Atlantic trade.

Sir John Brocklebank at the signing of the Q4 contract

As the jet airliner decimated transatlantic shipping, Cunard made plans for the future. Convinced it could still attract passengers to Atlantic liners in the jet age, the line set about designing a 75,000-ton, 1,000ft-long liner code-named Q3 – the third of the Queen-class liners.

A three-class design, with dimensions that made cruising impossible, Q3 followed in the wake of France's new flagship, SS *France*. *France* would have made a very fine liner in the golden age of transatlantic shipping. The longest liner ever built until *Queen Mary 2* in 2004, she was an elegant ship of state. However, her length, deep draft and ocean liner-style interior meant she was by no means designed for cruising. Her service on the North Atlantic was heavily subsidised by the French government as part of an ocean-going public relations exercise. The British government had no desire to subsidise a large British liner. As such, Cunard would have had to go it alone with Q3. As the situation facing the company worsened in the early 1960s, it re-evaluated the Q3 design, resulting in the project being cancelled on 19 October 1961.

The cash-strapped 122-year-old Cunard company was facing the harsh reality that, without a bold move and a change of direction, it would go out of business. To combat this threat, a new project was started. Code-named Q4, it called for a ship that was smaller than the existing Queens.

Q4 was 963ft in length, with a 105ft beam that would allow her to transit the Panama Canal, a 32ft draft, and the addition of bow thrusters that would make her suitable for cruising. The ship's superstructure design used an aluminium alloy. This lighter material allowed designers to add an extra deck

Mauretania (1939–65), despite her cruising conversion, was unsuccessful as a cruise ship and was ultimately retired. (Ian Boyle / Simplon Postcards)

QE2'S 40TH ANNIVERSARY

MICHAEL GALLAGHER

CUNARD PR AND OFFICIAL HISTORIAN

~~~

Given my interest in and love for *QE2*, which has spanned decades, it was a privilege to be so closely involved with her by handling PR for Cunard for many years. It was an honour to be responsible for her 40th anniversary celebrations in 2007.

By the time those celebrations took place it was known she only had just over a year of Cunard service left, but the affection and media interest was enormous and the 40th anniversary of her launch was still a celebration – a celebration of what was, quite simply, the finest ship sailing, the finest ship to fly the Cunard flag and the finest ship ever to sail.

Queen Mary departed Southampton for the final time on 31 October 1967. (Ian Boyle / Simplon Postcards)

Queen Elizabeth was retired from Cunard service in 1968 and was briefly opened as a tourist attraction in Fort Lauderdale. (Ian Boyle / Simplon Postcards)

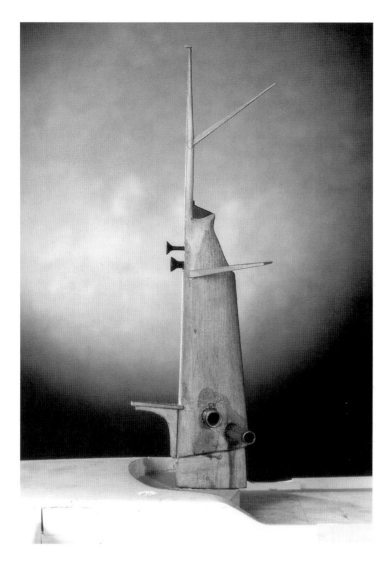

The original mast design for Q4. (Michael Gallagher / Cunard)

Various funnel designs were considered for *QE2*. (Michael Gallagher / Cunard)

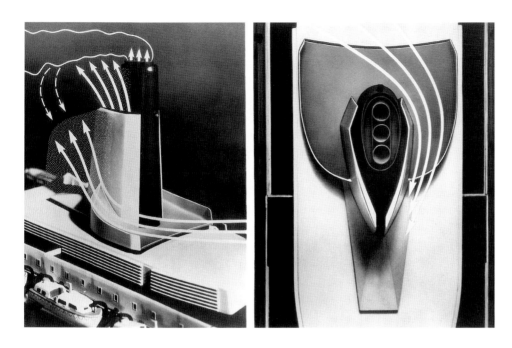

The ship's original funnel was designed to use the ship's forward motion to direct wind flow up the funnel casing causing soot to clear the aft decks. (Michael Gallagher / Cunard)

The design model of *QE2*'s original funnel. (Michael Gallagher / Cunard)

A cross-section of Q4 showing the layout of the internal spaces. (Michael Gallagher / Cunard)

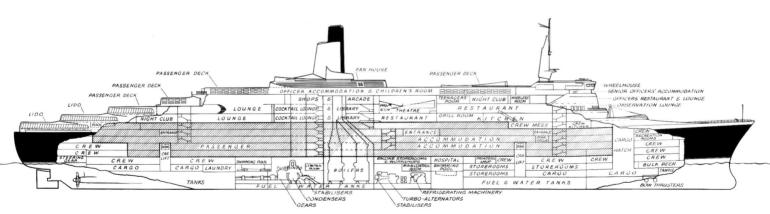

Q4 – the new 58,000 ton CUNARDER

The original profile model for *QE2*. (Michael Gallagher / Cunard)

compared with the design of the original Queens. Q4 was also a very different shape to previous Cunarders, with terraced lido decks, vast amounts of open deck space and multiple swimming pools – ideal for a cruising role. But the pivotal aspect of this ship was that, at her heart, she was an ocean liner. Q4's design called for a strong hull, long bow and a top speed of over 28.5 knots, allowing her to regularly complete the transatlantic crossing.

Cunard's commitment to Q4 and her more suitable cruise-focused dimensions allowed the company to apply for funding from the British government. The government saw the potential of Q4 and granted Cunard a £17.6 million loan. While

this made Q4 a realistic ambition, Cunard still had to mortgage eleven of its ships in order to raise a further £7.8 million to cover the cost of the build.

Tenders were called for Q4's construction on 9 September 1964, and on 30 December the contract was awarded to John Brown & Co. of Clydebank – the shipyard responsible for *Queen Mary* and *Queen Elizabeth*. The new ship was entered into the order book as 'Number 736', a name that the liner would be referred to throughout her construction. With the contract signed, work commenced at the shipyard to prepare the slipway for the laying of the keel, upon which the rest of the ship would be built.

four

SHIPS HAVE BEEN BORING LONG ENOUGH

The ultimate weapon against boredom at sea.

QE2 as described in a Cunard marketing brochure

In 1965 the use of prefabricated sections in shipbuilding was in its infancy, yet this method was used with *QE2*. The keel had been built in three welded sections, each weighing in at 60 tons. On the day of the keel-laying ceremony, these three sections were to be lifted into place in front of a crowd of journalists and photographers. Unfortunately the pieces were too large for the cranes to manage and the ceremony had to be aborted.

The keel was eventually laid on 5 July 1965 with much less fanfare. The build progressed much more slowly than anticipated. By March 1966 the ship was six months behind schedule, with further delays occurring as the build progressed. The delays were attributed to various causes including a shortage of skilled labour, strikes by various unions and changes to the design of the vessel. The launch date was pushed back from April 1967 to September 1967.

The timeframe of building the ship was not the only thing to blow out. By July 1967 it was clear that building costs would be more than £3 million over budget. Cunard appealed to the British government for an additional loan, which was granted, bringing the total government contribution to £24 million. This allowed work on the ship to continue.

The Queen launched the ship on 20 September 1967, with the words, 'I name this ship *Queen Elizabeth the Second*. May God

QE2 was built by John Brown & Co. of Clydebank. (Michael Gallagher / Cunard)

The bulbous bow is attached to *QE2*'s hull. (Michael Gallagher / Cunard)

Priming the hull is under way before the structure is completed. (Michael Gallagher / Cunard)

bless her and all who sail in her.' Following this announcement she used a pair of gold scissors to cut the ribbon holding the bottle of wine, which smashed on the bow: a propitious sign. The launch was accomplished with a press of a button, the ship finally taking to the water.

Cunard later consulted Buckingham Palace over the ship's name and was granted permission for the ship to be known as *Queen Elizabeth 2*, rather than using the Roman numeral II as was indicated by the naming ceremony.

Following the launch the ship was moved to the fitting out basin. And it was during the process of fitting out that the real differences in *QE2*'s design were to make themselves known. But fitting out was not without its own problems and delays. In January 1968, the John Brown Shipyard, which had sustained heavy losses during the construction of *QE2*, was amalgamated into Upper Clyde Shipbuilders. The engine works remained a separate company, which retained the name John Brown Engineering. Industrial actions continued to slow progress on the ship and it was with some relief on behalf of both Cunard and Upper Clyde Shipbuilders that the ship made her way down the Clyde for the first time on 19 November 1968. Prince Charles was on board for the short voyage and was given a tour of the ship, despite its unfinished condition.

Once the ship arrived in Greenock, the fitting out work continued. The ship's design, originally to be three-class as had been the case with the previous two Queens, was altered in the early stages to be a two-class design. When the ship was undertaking cruises, *QE2* would be run with a single class. The

Quarter Deck under construction. The section from Quarter Deck to Signal Deck was constructed from an aluminium alloy. (Michael Gallagher / Cunard)

QE2's stern ready for launch. (Michael Gallagher / Cunard)

HM the Queen, HRH the Duke of Edinburgh and shipyard director George Parker during a pre-launch inspection. (Michael Gallagher / Cunard)

The completed bow on launching day. (Michael Gallagher / Cunard)

HM the Queen prepares to cut the wire that released a bottle of Australian wine to christen the vessel. (Michael Gallagher / Cunard)

QE2 thunders down the slipway.
(Michael Gallagher / Cunard)

QE2's Bridge is craned aboard in April 1968. (Michael Gallagher / Cunard)

interior design work was to reflect the modern traveller. In its marketing material *QE2* was referred to as 'the ultimate weapon against boredom at sea', and slogans such as 'ships have been boring long enough' were used to demonstrate just how different this new ship was to be. Unlike the first two Queens, the interior was not to be art deco in design. Instead she was to be modern and sleek, a ship for the current times. The interiors made use of chrome and stainless steel. Fibreglass, leather and Formica were used extensively within to create easily cleaned surfaces that were also modern and fashionable.

The fitting out continued to suffer delays. In addition to industrial actions, there were cases of vandalism aboard and theft of materials from both the yard and the ship, including carpets, light fittings and copper piping. It was well known that *QE2* would be one of the last major builds on the Clyde, and as a result many workers and their unions wished to preserve their jobs for as long as possible, which did not encourage efficiency in the workforce.

Despite the incomplete nature of the interiors, the ship nevertheless proceeded to preliminary sea trials on 26 November 1968. Initially the trials appeared to be very successful. The ship was able to reach a speed of 29.5 knots,

which was very pleasing for both the yard and Cunard. However, the trials were abandoned and the ship returned to dry dock on 30 November, when an oil leak was identified in the high-pressure steam system. As a result of the leak the steam turbine system had to be thoroughly cleaned. The additional delay meant that the main sea trials had to be postponed and Cunard was forced to cancel the first of its planned cruises, a Christmas charity cruise.

The technical trials recommenced in mid December 1968, with the ship this time reaching a speed of 32.46 knots. The technical trials completed satisfactorily, the ship proceeded to acceptance trials. The acceptance trials involved a cruise to the Canary Islands, which would allow Cunard to fully test the air conditioning and the machinery. In addition the passenger services were also to be tested, with passengers ordering from the menu and participating in daily activities. Travelling aboard the ship were more than 500 members of Cunard staff and their families.

On this journey *QE2* also carried around 200 members of the fitting out crew, who were still hard at work trying to complete the ship's interiors. This was not to be the worst of the problems, as first the starboard and then the port

Thousands of spectators watched QE2 being launched on 20 September 1967. (Michael Gallagher / Cunard)

The lower section of the funnel is hoisted into position. (Michael Gallagher / Cunard)

The completed funnel as seen from Signal Deck. (Michael Gallagher / Cunard)

Painting is under way on *QE2*'s aft decks. (Michael Gallagher / Cunard)

Captain Bil Warwick on the ship's starboard Bridge wing.
(Michael Gallagher / Cunard)

REFURBISHING *QE2*

CAPTAIN CHRIS WELLS

~~~~

My biggest memories of refit on *QE2* go back to 1994 – the infamous 'disaster refit' in Hamburg, where we came out unfinished! But actually, this was a very interesting refit, as the ship went in as an iconic modern vessel of the 1960s, complete with multicoloured Formica-clad stair towers, and came out as a classical liner of bygone eras, with real wood veneered stair towers! We added the new Yacht Club and created the Lido dining area aft, removing one pool in the process (the Lido kitchen went in the space released). The amount of work attempted to refurbish all the bathrooms exceeded the available man-hours, and was one of the main reasons why the refurbishment work was not completed on time. My role during that refit was as 'tank-man'! Out of sight of everybody, and in the bowels of the ship, we conducted significant steelwork repairs to the ballast tanks. That bit we completed successfully!

Between 1996 and 1998 I was assigned to *Royal Viking Sun*, returning to *QE2* as staff captain in 1999, ready for that refit which was in Bremerhaven … and my main memory of that one was that we sandblasted the entire hull (taking off many old layers of paint, as she hadn't been blasted for many years) and recoated her in Cunard's traditional federal grey.

As the ship was about to enter the dry dock, Greenpeace protesters tried to prevent her going in by tying themselves together in a chain across the entrance to the dock. (The protest was about the content of the TBT paint that was to be blasted off the hull.) So the ship was put alongside an adjacent berth, where many of our surplus crew were disembarked (they were hurrying for booked flights home) and while attention of the media was concentrated on what was happening on the shore side of our ship, the authorities were forcibly removing the protesters from the water on the other side … We docked a few hours later than planned!

high-pressure turbine suffered malfunctions. It was determined to send *QE2* to Southampton for repair and completion, as it was much closer than the Clyde. With no firm delivery date possible, Cunard was forced to cancel the planned and booked January cruises, at considerable loss of income, issuing the following statement:

Captain Bil Warwick and Cunard Chairman Sir Basil Smallpeice with Prince Charles during *QE2*'s short voyage to Greenock. (Michael Gallagher / Cunard)

Cunard cannot accept delivery until after the ship's turbines have been thoroughly retested and proved in further basin trials and sea trials and a prolonged acceptance trial under

The completed *QE2*.
(Michael Gallagher /
Cunard)

maintained pressure, followed by further inspection. It is impossible to say when this programme of correction, testing and proving of the ship's power can be completed.

Once the ship was in Southampton, the turbines were inspected and it was found that many of the blades had sheared off, damaging other blades and the nozzle passages of the turbines. This was not a situation that could be quickly fixed;

it required extensive repairs and replacement blades. Over the following months this repair work was performed and the interiors were completed. At the end of March the ship underwent and passed her sea trials, with the acceptance trial from 30 March to 7 April also being successful. On 18 April 1969 *QE2* was finally handed over to Cunard.

five

CELEBRATION AND CAUTION

Ladies and gentlemen, we have received information concerning a threat of a bomb explosion on board this ship some time during this voyage.

Captain William Law

QE2 departed on her first passenger service on 22 April 1969. The voyage was an eight-day round-trip cruise to the Canary Islands. Following her return to Southampton she was made ready for her maiden transatlantic crossing.

The day before QE2 departed on her first transatlantic voyage, the Queen and Duke of Edinburgh visited the ship. They were shown around the ship by her captain, Bil Warwick, and also partook of lunch.

The next day QE2 departed Southampton bound for Le Havre and then New York. Many fireboats and other small craft congregated to celebrate the occasion. She was given a warm welcome in Le Havre with many onlookers turning out to see the new Queen.

The crossing from Le Havre to New York was accomplished at an average speed of just over 28 knots. The total time was four days, sixteen hours and thirty-five minutes – a not unimpressive feat. Her arrival in New York did not go unnoticed. Dozens of pleasure craft, a coastguard ship and a navy destroyer came out to meet her. Press photographers were in evidence and various dignitaries, including the mayor, paid the ship a visit. The ship spent two days in New York before setting sail for Southampton.

Cunard could finally breathe a sigh of relief. Its new ship was a success. QE2's early voyages were well booked. Throughout the summer months she maintained a regular transatlantic schedule, with the ship carrying 25,000 passengers by August 1969. The ship had also proven its seaworthiness, having weathered several severe storms on her Atlantic crossings. As the weather on the Atlantic turned worse, it was time for QE2 to prove herself as a cruise ship.

The 1969–70 winter season involved a series of ten-day Caribbean cruises. Returning from one of these cruises on 5 February 1970, the ship was met with an ice-filled New York Harbor coupled with a tug strike. It took four attempts to dock QE2 at Pier 92 without the aid of tugs, and required the smashing of the ice with the ship's hull in order to get in. Captain Bil Warwick said of the event, 'I never thought I would have to use a £30 million ship as an ice-breaker.'

While on a Caribbean cruise on 8 January 1971, QE2 was called to the aid of the French liner Antilles, which had caught fire after running aground on a reef off the coast of Mustique in the Grenadines. The passengers were evacuated and brought ashore in Mustique and Bequia. At the time QE2 was anchored off the island of St Lucia. On hearing the distress call, the ship made its way to the stricken liner, arriving after dark to find the Antilles ablaze and grounded. QE2 was able to take aboard the evacuated passengers and crew of Antilles from Mustique, and sailed for Barbados. Once there, most of the rescued people

BRITANNIA GRILL RESTAURANT

QUEEN ELIZABETH 2
CUNARD

2001 World Cruise – En Route to Bali
Sunday 18th February, 2001

SIMPLICITY

With today's changing lifestyles and the quest for healthier living through increased nutritional awareness, we at Cunard, bring you a daily selection of dishes, that reflect these needs. These dishes, although low in cholesterol, salt and fat, are high in flavour.

Vegetable Crudités with Low Fat Cream Cheese Dip

*

Beef Consommé with Carrots and Chives

*

Radicchio Salad with Your Choice of Fat Free Dressing

*

Ginger Pesto Crusted Fresh Opakapaka Fillet
With Coconut Cream Sauce, Snow Peas, Mushroom - Corn Rice and Pineapple Mango Relish

*

SUGAR FREE - Profiteroles with Tropical Fruits Salsa

A Selection of Steamed Vegetables and Baked Potatoes are Always Available

A LA CARTE

Smoked Salmon Rose with Sevruga Caviar
Thinly Sliced Parma Ham with Seasonal Melon
Caesar Salad with Garlic Crôutons and Parmesan Shavings
Baked Fillet of Norwegian Salmon
Whole Dover Sole Grilled or Meunière with New Potatoes
Crisp Chicken Breast with Rosemary
Gri... ngus Beef Fillet Steak, Madagascar Pepper Sauce

All dis...

Klaus ...
Chef d...

DINNER

APPETIZERS
Smoked Trout with Mini Baked Potato and Chive Sour Cream
Caesar Salad with Grilled Chicken Breast
Seafood Crepes on Sautéed Fresh Spinach, Gratinated with Hollandaise
Deep Fried Mushrooms, Stuffed with Cheddar Cheese and Smoked Ham, Garlic Dip

SOUPS
Slow Roasted Garlic Soup with Rye Bread Crôutons
Beef Bouillon with Angel Hair Pasta and Chervil
Chilled Apple and Peach Soup with Cider

SALADS
Radicchio in Sweet Honey Mustard Dressing
Grilled Eggplant Drizzled with Mint Garlic Yoghurt

A TASTE OF THE MEDITERRANEAN
Spaghetti all Pomodoro
Italian Pasta with Tomato and Fresh Basil Sauce, Grated Parmesan Cheese

ENTRÉES
Ginger Pesto Crusted Fresh Red Emperor Fillet
With Coconut Cream Sauce, Snow Peas, Corn Rice and Pineapple Mango Relish
Fresh Black Mussels in White Wine and Shallot, Parsley, Toasted Garlic Baguette
Roast Milk Fed Veal Loin with Sautéed Wild Mushrooms, Rosemary Jus
Risotto Primavera and Vegetables in Season
Grilled Prime Beef Sirloin Steak with Four Pepper Sauce
Lyonnaise Potatoes, Asparagus and Paty Pan Squash
Sautéed Pheasant Breast with Madeira and Grape Sauce
Braised Savoy Cabbage, Pommes Williams and Roasted Turnips

VEGETARIA...
Thai Eggplant Curry wi...

"Public Health Services have determined ...
cooked meat, poultry, fish, seafood or eggs may...

YOUR SOMMELI...
Beringer "Private Reserve" C...
Joseph Phelps Cabernet Sau...

Queen Elizabeth 2
1995 Golden Route World Cruise

QUEEN ELIZABETH 2
CUNARD

WORLD CRUISE
1998

GRAND PASSAGE TO DISTANT LANDS

VOYAGE OF DISCOVERY
QE2
2003 WORLD CRUISE
CUNARD

MAURETANIA RES...

QUEEN ELIZABETH 2
CUNARD

2003 World Cruise – In the Port of Auckland
Wednesday 5th February 2003

FITNESS SPA SUGGESTION

Mixed Garden Greens with Your Choice of Fat Free Dressing

~

Celery Bouillon with Vermicelli

~

Poached Chicken Breast in Vegetable Court Boullion

~

Chilled Fresh Fruit Plate

TO ACCOMPANY YOUR MEAL

2000	Benziger Chardonnay, by the glass	$6.00
1999	Estancia, Cabernet Sauvignon, by the glass	$6.00

Nizam Nor
Chef de Cuisine

Ico Pranic
Maitre D' Hotel

CUNARD
Queen Elizabeth 2

Captain John Burton-Hall, R.D.*, R.N.R.

cordially invites all passengers
who embarked in Suva and Auckland
to join him and his officers for cocktails
on Monday, 6th February
in the Queen's Room at 7.15pm.

(Please enter via the portside by the Library)   Dress: Formal

QUEEN ELIZABETH 2

Passenger Name _____
# of Bags _____
Hotel _____

41

...ETANIA RESTAURANT

QUEEN ELIZABETH 2
CUNARD

World Cruise Voyage of Discovery – En Route to Fremantle
Wednesday 16th February, 2005

SIMPLICITY

With today's changing lifestyles and the quest for healthier living through increased nutritional awareness, we at Cunard, bring you a daily selection of dishes, that reflect these needs. These dishes, although low in cholesterol, salt and fat, are high in flavour.

Grilled Eggplant and Yellow Squash Slices, Marinated with Fresh Thyme and Olive Oil

Chicken Consommé with Vegetables

Bitter Lettuce and Herb Salad with Balsamic Vinegar and Virgin Olive Oil
Ranch, Blue Cheese, Caesar, Thousand Island, Italian and French Dressing

Salmon Piccata on Linguini Pasta, Sautéed Mushrooms, Tomato Coulis and Broccoli

Sugar-Free Figs and Lemon Tart

A Selection of Steamed Vegetables and Baked Potatoes are always available

VEGETARIAN
Melanzane Parmigiana al Forno
Oven Baked Eggplant Parmigiana

YOUR SOM...
2002   Pinot Bianco, Alois ...
1999   Antinori Chianti Cl...

Josef Reitstaetter
Chef de Cuisine

ITALIAN DINNER

APPETIZERS
Terrina ai Frutti di Mare con Marinata alle Safferano
Terrine with Rock Lobster, Monkfish and Shrimps - Saffron Vinaigrette
...pasto-Melanzane Alla Griglia, Grissini con Salame, Pomodoro Moz...
...ipasto - Grilled Eggplant, Salami on Grissini Stick, Tomato Mozzarella, Artichokes...
Vitello Tonnato - Vitello con Salsa al Tonno
Vitello Tonnato - Thinly Sliced Veal in Tuna Sauce

SOUPS
Fagioli Bianchi con Olio al Tartufo Piemontese
Cream Soup of White Beans with Piemontese Truffle Oil
Minestrone Zuppa di Verdure
Italian Vegetable Soup
Uva Fresca con Yoghurt
Chilled Grapes with Yogurt

SALAD
Insalata di Verdura Mista con Erbe All'Acetoa
Mixed Raw Vegetable Salad with Herb Vinaigrette

ENTRÉES
Penne Rigate alla Puttanesca
Italian Pasta with Olives, Anchovies, Capers, Garlic and Tomato Sauce
Piccata di Salmone con Pancetta e Linguine
Salmon Piccata in Pancetta Ham on Linguini Pasta, Sautéed Mushrooms, Tomato Cou...
Ossobuco "Gremolata" di Vitello Brasato con Gnocchi alla Ro...
Braised Veal Shank with Buttered Broccoli and sautéed Yellow Squas...
Tournedos "Rossini" alla Griglia con Pate di Fegato e Salsa al...
Grilled Beef Tournedo on Crouton with Foie Gras, Truffle Sauce...
Asparagus, Vegetable Bouquet in Tomato and Dauphin Potatoes...

SWEET INDULGENCE
Torta al Marzapane con Salsa all'Amaretto - Marzipan Cake with A...
Tiramisu con Salsa Al Kahlua - Tiramisu with Kahlua and...
Zabaglione al Marsala con Savoiardi - Marsala Zabaglione with...
Sugar-Free Fig and Lemon Tart

SORBET   **ICE CREAM**   **FROZEN YOGHURT**
Orange Campari   Vanilla   Banana
   Toasted Almond
   Strawberry

ASSORTED INTERNATIONAL CHEESE
Bread Selection and Crackers

CUNARD'S SELECTION OF
Exotic Teas
Espresso, Cappuccino
Regular and Decaffeinated Coffee

PETITS FOURS

LUNCHEON
HOME MADE BREAD FROM OUR BAKER'S SHOP

STARTERS
Seafood Salad with a Light Oriental Dressing
Cold Roast Beef Rolls Filled with Goose Liver Mousse, Apple-Orange C...
Mexican Spicy Beef and Bean Soup
Chilled Tangerine Soup
Mixed Garden Greens with Your Choice of Home Made Dressing

A TASTE OF ITALY
Saffron Fettuccini
Italian Pasta with Tomatoes, Goats Cheese, Red Onion and Bell Pepper

MAIN COURSES FROM CHEF BERNARD'S RECIPES
Freshly made Salmon Cakes on Salad Bouquet with Remoulade Sauce
Honey and Pineapple Roasted Gammon Ham
Brussels Sprouts Paysanne, Scallion Mashed Potatoes and Madeira Sauce
Traditional Beef Stew, in Rich Paprika Onion Sauce
Served with small Homemade Bread Dumpling or Steamed Potato
Poached Egg on Smoked Haddock with Cheddar Cheese Sauce
Vegetarian - Spinach Lasagna with Courgette and Pecorino Cheese

FROM THE BARBEQUE GRILL
All Beef Hot Dog
Hamburger or Cheeseburger
Minute Steak, Herb Butter
Chicken Satay with Red and Green Thai Curry Dipping Sauce

PANTRY CHEF'S RECOMMENDATION
Parisienne Style Fried Plaice Fillet on Scotch Soft Roll Bap
Boston Leaves and Curried Mayonnaise Potato Salad
Heart of Iceberg Lettuce with Curried Egg and Cress Salad with Cooked Ham
Roast Venison Loin with Lingonberry Mousse and Marinated Chanterelles
A Variety of International Cheeses and Crackers

FOR THE SWEET TOOTH
Wild Berry Flan with Vanilla Sauce
Sticky Toffee Pudding, Caramel Sauce
...oup Peach Melba - Vanilla Ice Cream with Peach in Syrup and Raspberry Sauce
Sugar Free Banana and Chocolate Filo Strudel with Warm Vanilla Sauce

FROM THE ICE CREAM PARLOUR
SORBET   **ICE CREAM**   **FROZEN YOGHURT**   **SAUCES**
Kiwi   Vanilla   Raspberry   Caramel
   Chocolate   Pineapp...

AP   005347

PASSENGER TICKET
& PASSAGE CONTRACT
CUNARD

IMPORTANT PLEASE READ FOLLOWING TERMS OF PASSAGE CONTRACT:
For valuable consideration, Cunard Line Limited,
hereinafter referred to as the "Company", agrees to provide (continued on page 3)

Right: The Lookout Bar was quintessentially 1960s in style. (Michael Gallagher / Cunard)

Far right: The Grill Room on Quarter Deck displayed statues by Janine Janet. (Michael Gallagher / Cunard)

Below: The Columbia restaurant on Quarter Deck was the first-class restaurant. (Michael Gallagher / Cunard)

QE2's mast was 21.2m (69ft 6in) tall. (Michael Gallagher / Cunard)

The mast and funnel both appeared much taller prior to the addition of the balcony suites on the Signal and Sports (later Sun) Decks in 1972. (Michael Gallagher / Cunard)

disembarked, except for eighty-five guests who chose to stay aboard and complete their cruise on QE2!

By October 1969 Cunard had repaid £2.5 million of its government loan, with plans to repay a further £500,000 every six months thereafter. But the company's finances were by no means as stable as it would have liked. A number of outside issues, including a recession in the United States and greatly increased fuel costs, took their toll, and the line posted a loss of £1.9 million in 1970. With losses projected to continue and no clear way for the line to recover as an independent company, it was not a complete surprise when in August 1971 Trafalgar House purchased Cunard, and QE2, for £27.3 million. The final board meeting as an independent company was held on 25 August 1971. Trafalgar House owned a number of companies in many different fields, and the public wondered what impact the purchase of the company would have on QE2. The group was quick to reassure the public that Cunard would continue to operate as a shipping company and that QE2 would continue to sail under the British ensign. In fact Trafalgar House was convinced that QE2 was going to be a great success

The Lookout Bar on Upper Deck had a forward-facing view. (Michael Gallagher / Cunard)

The Lookout Bar was removed during the 1972 refit. (Michael Gallagher / Cunard)

and undertook a total survey of the ship and her services soon after purchasing Cunard. As a result of this survey the group made plans for a sweeping renovation of the ship, including the addition of balcony penthouse accommodation on the Signal and Sports (later Sun) Decks.

In May 1972 the ship made headlines when a suspicious telephone call was received at the New York office. The caller demanded US$350,000 and, if Cunard refused, he threatened to detonate explosives aboard *QE2*. At the time, *QE2* was at sea with 2,150 passengers and crew aboard. She was under the command of Captain William Law who, once notified by Cunard, organised a security sweep of the ship, which did not yield any results. Nonetheless Cunard decided the risk was too great to ignore and, working with the authorities, agreed to pay the ransom. Concurrently, Scotland Yard and the British Ministry of Defence were alerted and opted to send bomb-disposal experts to rendezvous with *QE2*.

With a plan in place, Captain Law addressed *QE2*'s passengers and crew:

THE BOMB SCARE

COMMODORE JOHN BURTON-HALL

Chris and Rachelle have written about our 1972 bomb scare in the Atlantic. As junior first officer, I recall the arrival on the Bridge of the Royal Marine officer who had escorted the bomb-disposal officer of the team, who had just heroically parachuted into the cold waters of the North Atlantic for the first and, hopefully, only time in his life. The officer marched into the wheelhouse up to Captain Law, unzipped his wetsuit, and produced that day's copy of *The Times*, with the words, 'I'm sorry, Sir; this was all I could find in the mess.'

QE2 in her original 1969 configuration. (Michael Gallagher / Cunard)

QE2 was designed to allow her to enter the shallower cruise ports of the Caribbean. (Michael Gallagher / Cunard)

Ladies and Gentlemen, we have received information concerning a threat of a bomb explosion on board this ship some time during this voyage. We have received such threats in the past, which have so far turned out to be hoaxes. However, we always take them seriously and take every possible precaution.

On this occasion we are being assisted by the British Government who are sending out bomb disposal experts who will be parachuted into the sea and picked up by boat and brought aboard.

I will of course keep you fully informed about the situation. Cunard are taking every precaution ashore and on board and will take any necessary action to minimise risk. If there is any question of it being necessary to pay over money, this will be done ashore in New York.

I can only ask you to remain calm. On these occasions lots of rumours tend to circulate. Please only take notice of any information that comes from me directly or from one of my officers. That is all for the moment.

QE2 at speed, looking smart in her original configuration. (Michael Gallagher / Cunard)

Visiting warm and tropical locations made *QE2* popular with people escaping the northern winter. (Michael Gallagher / Cunard)

A Royal Air Force Nimrod jet was sent out to provide air reconnaissance while a four-man bomb-disposal unit parachuted from a Royal Air Force C-130 Hercules. They were met by two of *QE2*'s lifeboats and brought aboard the ship, and all the while *QE2*'s passengers lined the decks to watch the spectacle. Despite a thorough sweep of *QE2*, no explosives were found and the ship continued her journey to Cherbourg and Southampton safely. Meanwhile, in New York Cunard worked with the FBI in an attempt to capture the perpetrator. To that end, the company made the cash drop, with the FBI closely monitoring the location. However, no one arrived to collect the money and it was returned to the company the following day. The next month, the culprit was arrested for making threats to *QE2* and American Airlines, and was sentenced to twenty years in prison. The incident had a long-lasting effect on *QE2*: public visits to the ship stopped as a result of the heightened security measures that were introduced aboard the liner.

QE2'S ODD STAIRWAYS

QE2 had eight main stairways, labelled A (forward) to H (aft). Compared with modern cruise ships, which generally have just two or three stairways, you could be forgiven for thinking that *QE2*'s eight options gave passengers easy access to her various decks and public rooms. But you'd be wrong: *QE2* entered service as a two-class ship and, rather than using gates and barriers to segregate the classes as on older transatlantic liners, *QE2*'s designers used the stairways to 'keep everyone in their place' in a more subtle way. A series of stairways linked the first-class areas with first-class accommodation and tourist-class areas with tourist-class accommodation.

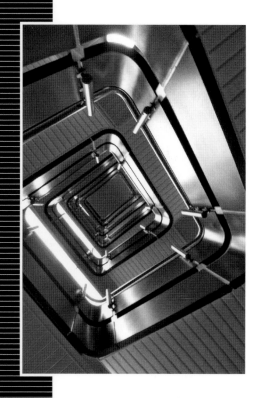

E Stairway, looking up.
(Frame / Cross)

For example, the A Stairway had no landings on Quarter Deck or One Deck, while B Stairway spanned only from Two Deck to Five Deck and was designed to facilitate movement from the tourist-class quarters at the forward ends of this deck. C Stairway linked the Princess Grill on Quarter Deck with its lounge on One Deck, but also descended as far as the medical centre on Six Deck and the indoor pool on Seven Deck, while F Stairway linked the Purser's Office on Two Deck to the QE2 Spa on Six Deck. H Stairway performed a similar function as B Stairway for tourist-class passengers at the aft end of the ship. D and G Stairways linked most of the ship, although in the case of the D Stairway the elevators only linked Boat Deck to Three Deck (first-class areas), while those on Four and Five Decks had to take the stairs. G Stairway linked passenger decks from Upper Deck to Five Deck, with a spiral stairway between Upper Deck and Boat Deck.

If you wanted to get to all the main passenger decks aboard *QE2*, you would head for E Stairway. Here, four banks of lifts and twin stairwells spanned Boat Deck to Five Deck with regular passengers aware that 'E' stood for 'everywhere'.

The seeming chaos of *QE2*'s stairways was further exacerbated by the addition of the balcony suites to Signal and Sun Decks, accessible only through a completely separate stairway and lift from the Queens Grill Lounge.

Still, despite the initial confusion, one of the joys of *QE2* was working out how to get around the ship – with many options to get from point A to point B around the vessel. This, coupled by a myriad of corridors across all the main decks, meant regular *QE2* travellers were often saving lost newcomers.

six

CHANGING COURSE

I wish her God speed, and you and your officers and crew every success in adding to the 1 million miles already sailed.

HM the Queen on the 10th anniversary of *QE2* entering service

By October 1972 *QE2* was ready for her first Trafalgar House refit. Work was undertaken at Vosper Thorneycroft in Southampton, however workmen actually boarded *QE2* during her summer Atlantic season to commence preliminary works on the ship. Particular attention was taken to precise measurements of *QE2*'s top decks to ensure the prefabricated balcony cabins would fit perfectly when craned aboard the ship in Southampton. Other changes to the ship included the creation of the Queens Grill and Queens Grill Lounge as well as a dedicated galley. These rooms replaced a coffee shop, jukebox room, casino and nightclub. The Britannia restaurant (later Mauretania) was expanded and a new galley built in the area formerly occupied by the Lookout Bar. This included the addition of a box-like structure on *QE2*'s forward superstructure that housed the vegetable preparation room, a refuse chute and a lift that linked the galley with the storerooms many decks below. The Columbia restaurant (later Caronia) was given the sole use of the original galley, which underwent its own refit. The Columbia restaurant was expanded, taking over space originally dedicated to the Grill Room on the port side of the ship. This expansion allowed it to seat over 800 people. The Double Down Room (later Grand Lounge) also underwent some changes during the refit. The shops were moved to the top floor and the stage was extended, with the overall capacity

The Signal and Sports (later Sun) Decks balcony accommodation was built from prefabricated sections. (Commodore R.W. Warwick, *QE2: The Cunard Flagship Queen Elizabeth II*)

Balcony accommodation was added to the ship in 1972 whilst alongside in Southampton. (Commodore R.W. Warwick, *QE2: The Cunard Flagship Queen Elizabeth II*)

The Queens Grill was added in 1972 to serve the newly created balcony suites. (Michael Gallagher / Cunard)

In 1972 the Shopping Promenade was relocated to the upper level of the Double Down Room. (Michael Gallagher / Cunard)

MARRIAGE

COMMODORE JOHN BURTON-HALL

~~~

On 30 December 1980 I was staff captain as the ship sailed from Martinique on a Caribbean cruise. On board was an actress with her theatre company performing plays by, among others, George Bernard Shaw and Nöel Coward. I proposed after seventeen minutes, perhaps a record, but have since wondered what took me so long.

Still on marriage, but fast-forwarding to the 1994 50th anniversary of the D-Day Landings, when I was in command of QE2 bringing American army veterans and their wives across the Atlantic. Some of these ladies were GI brides, and had not been back to the UK since the end of the war. They shared their treasured memories with us, and jitterbugged around the Grand Lounge with the recaptured *joie de vivre* of their younger selves.

of the room also being increased. The total cost of the renovations was £1.8 million. Despite a delay in delivery of the ship, the changes were well received by passengers.

With *QE2* back in service, Cunard and Trafalgar House were keen to leverage the positive media response to her refurbishment and further build the ship's reputation. As a result, in 1973 the iconic liner was chartered by Assured Travel Massachusetts for two special voyages between Southampton and Israel to celebrate that nation's 25th anniversary. However, this presented a unique series of challenges. Tensions in the Middle East meant that *QE2* would be a high-value target for enemies of Israel. As such, planning for the voyage was complex, involving a variety of agencies, including the British Ministry of Defence. The risks also resulted in a lower than expected passenger complement on the voyage, with *QE2* carrying just over 600 passengers to and from Israel. Furthermore, the National Union of Seaman negotiated 'danger pay' for *QE2*'s crew in compensation for the treacherous waters the liner was sailing into.

The return voyages were completed safely. However, the following year Egyptian president Anwar Sadat revealed in a BBC interview that he had countermanded an order to sink *QE2*! The order had been issued to an Egyptian submarine by President Gaddafi of Libya, to avenge the loss of Libyan Arab Airlines LN114, which had been shot down by Israel in February 1973. With Egypt and Libya sharing arms at the time, the order could well have been carried out had the Egyptian captain not opted to confirm the orders with his superiors; luckily, President Sadat stepped in.

Later that year, all three of *QE2*'s boilers failed, resulting in a catastrophic power failure that affected all parts of the liner. Lighting, refrigeration, air conditioning, the galleys, elevators, fresh water production and pumping all ceased to work. The situation lasted for more than a day, with passengers becoming understandably concerned about the plight of the ship. Rescue came in the form of *Sea Venture* (later *Pacific Princess* of *The Love Boat* fame). At 19,900 gross tons, *Sea Venture* was much smaller than *QE2*, but she was given a special licence to carry 1,000 of *QE2*'s 1,400 passengers to Bermuda. *QE2* was later towed to Hamilton, Bermuda,

The refurbished *QE2* at sea sporting her new balcony suites. (Michael Gallagher / Cunard)

A forward view of *QE2* shows the altered forward profile with observation windows removed. (Michael Gallagher / Cunard)

This photo shows the original aft deck configuration. (Michael Gallagher / Cunard)

Above: The Queen Mary suite is craned aboard *QE2* during the 1977 refit. (Michael Gallagher / Cunard)

Right: *QE2* returns to service following her 1977 refit. (Michael Gallagher / Cunard)

THE UNVEILING

COMMODORE JOHN BURTON-HALL

~~~

Still suffering the indignity of her 1994 refit, and with work still carrying on around us, *QE2* hosted a visit from HRH the Duke of York before setting off on her Christmas cruise. I had managed to retrieve, from the parlour of the Mayor of Southampton, a large portrait of the Queen and the Duke of Edinburgh, together with another large portrait of the Queen Mother, which had originally hung in the ship. These were duly displayed in the Queens Room, covered with heavy red drapes, awaiting unveiling by the Duke, whose familiar good humour was also about to be revealed. Having already pointed out earlier in the day the flimsiness of the bar which supported these drapes and requested a stronger version, I confidently arrived with His Royal Highness and asked him if he would kindly, as planned, reveal the paintings to the assembled VIPs, travel agents and media who, mercifully, had not been allowed cameras or recording equipment. The ensuing flourish dislodged the shaky bar, which, in it's skew-whiff vertical passage, missed us by a hair's breadth, with accompanying drapes landing fetchingly on our heads and shoulders, presenting us as two figures in an unfinished painting by an unknown, unsuccessful follower of Caravaggio.

Left and right: *QE2* transiting the Panama Canal on her 1979 World Cruise. (Michael Gallagher / Cunard)

BARONESS P.D. JAMES

CARMEL RODGERS
QE2 BOOKSHOP MANAGER

~~~

Baroness P.D. James was the much acclaimed and popular authoress of many books, including *Shroud for a Nightingale*, *Death of an Expert Witness*, *Devices and Desires*, *The Children of Men* ... She signed her autobiographical *Time to be in Earnest* with, 'To Carmel, with many thanks for all your help and with warm good wishes. P.D. James, 29 Sept. 2003.'

I had the pleasure of meeting her on two occasions when she was 'Author on Board' of *QE2*, when I presided over the bookshop.

She obligingly agreed to a book signing, and for a good few hours beforehand her titles were flying off the shelves like hot cakes! Baroness James sat and signed the books of her fans for more than two hours. It was the longest book signing I could remember. The lines of fans, stretched from her table, down Quarter Deck past the Cruise Sales office, did a U-turn at the entrance to the Caronia restaurant and stretched back past the Chartroom Bar right along to halfway down the Queens Room.

Now please remember Baroness James was born in the 1920s and, although very spry, she was not a young woman. I was worried about the state of her signing hand – she was indefatigable – and when I asked if I could get her anything, she smiled and asked me if I could pad her fountain pen with a tissue, as her hand was aching and her fingers were losing their grip. She also told me, 'I could murder a glass of red wine'.

With her wine at her side and her pen wrapped in a tissue, she signed and chatted and chatted and signed until the very last person was thanked and their book was autographed. It was a marathon! She remained utterly charming, before, during and after the entire book signing.

Afterwards, I escorted her along to the stern of the ship to the Lido restaurant, where she was going to 'have a little snack'. She thanked me and I could not help but give her a hug. Baroness James was a trouper and a treasure.

The second time she came aboard was a repeat of the same process. Her popularity being as it is, she was again inundated with requests as she signed her books – and once again the line went around the ship.

I doubt very much if she would have remembered me – she must have done thousands of book signings – but I have fond memories of time spent with a real lady, which I will never forget.

Post-1977 *QE2*'s profile had been altered again. Note the new Queen Mary and Queen Elizabeth suites aft of her mast. (Michael Gallagher / Cunard)

where she was repaired. But issues with both boilers and turbines would continue to dog the liner until the mid 1980s.

Throughout her career, *QE2* was well known globally due to her annual world cruises, undertaken during the northern hemisphere's winter months. They usually spanned 90 to 100 days and saw *QE2* visit ports as far afield as Sydney, Cape Town and Yokohama. *QE2*'s first world cruise occurred in 1975. Planning for the voyage took almost two years, and included sending Captain Woodall around the world to inspect individual ports to ensure they could cope with both the liner's size and her status as the most famous ship in the world. This voyage included *QE2*'s first ever transit of the Panama Canal, which occurred on 25 March 1975 and saw the ship become the then largest ship to have used the canal. That same year, *QE2*'s odometer clocked 1 million nautical miles.

The next two years were plagued with problems for *QE2*. A serious engine room fire resulted in significant damage to one of the turbines. The fire's intense heat, ventilating up the exhaust pipes, also caused visible damage to her funnel. Then, in late 1976, *QE2*'s bow anchor was dislodged from its housing and fell into the sea during stormy weather. The anchor tore a hole in *QE2*'s bulbous bow, resulting in flooding, which led to the voyage being diverted to Boston.

These incidents, as well as general wear and tear, led to *QE2* undergoing another significant refurbishment in 1977. This refit was undertaken in the United States at the Bethlehem Steel Corporation Shipyard in New Jersey, and included the addition of the Queen Elizabeth and Queen Mary suites to the forward end of Signal Deck. They were built on the dockside and craned aboard once *QE2* arrived in New Jersey. These

TAKING *QE2* TO SEA

COMMODORE JOHN BURTON-HALL

The first time I took *QE2* to sea as master was sailing from Hong Kong to Japan. As junks darted to and fro like fireflies, I was constantly reminded of the days I sailed these waters with the Blue Funnel Line, when we were well aware that a Chinese fisherman's idea of good luck was to have sailed as close as possible across the bows of a large vessel.

Commodore John Burton-Hall first took command of QE2 in 1990. (Michael Gallagher / Cunard)

One of the many *QE2* lifebuoys found on Boat Deck. (Frame / Cross)

split-level suites offered balcony views over the side of *QE2* and a unique forward perspective, and were quite simply the finest accommodation at sea. They were the only American-made parts of *QE2*'s superstructure. Other work included rebuilding and renaming the tourist-class restaurant as Tables of the World. This remodelling saw the area divided into themed zones representing the UK, France, Italy, Spain and Asia.

That same year, *QE2* was partnered with the British Airways Concorde to offer a unique transatlantic experience. Passengers sailed across the Atlantic in a leisurely five-day crossing aboard *QE2* before returning home aboard Concorde in just over three hours – or vice versa. This partnership, along with Cunard's revised focus on cruising and world voyages, saw *QE2* and Cunard return a respectable profit in 1977 – so much so that the world voyage was repeated in 1978 and became an annual event on *QE2*'s schedule.

In May 1979 Cunard celebrated the 10th anniversary of *QE2* entering service with a special cruise. To mark the occasion, Captain Bob Arnott sent a message to HM the Queen, to which she replied, 'I wish her Godspeed and you and your officers and crew every success in adding to the 1 million miles already sailed.' This historic voyage was followed by *QE2*'s first transit of the Suez Canal in 1980 as part of her world cruise. All eyes turned to *QE2* during that voyage when she docked in Yalta, which was under Soviet control. The visit was not successful: a stand-off between Soviet officials and *QE2*'s officers resulted in the Cunard flagship weighing anchor and leaving before the first passenger reached the shore.

'I STILL MISS *QE2*'

BILL MILLER

MARITIME HISTORIAN AND *QE2* LECTURER

QE2 has to be among my favourite liners – and one that I made something close to fifty trips aboard – transalantic as well as cruises to Bermuda, Norway, eastern Canada, the Caribbean and trans-Panama Canal. My very first trip was nearly fifty years ago, in November 1970. The ship was returning from her very first long cruise, Europe–Africa–South America, and I joined for the last five days, coming north from the Caribbean to New York. The ship was still quite new and therefore exciting – and the voyage itself was done in high style.

I recall *Gone with the Wind* being shown in the theatre in two parts. I also recall that, despite her being the new $80 million Cunard flagship, the company had obviously found a supply of red plastic swizzle sticks to be used in the bars. They all read 'Cunard–White Star', a title not used since 1950. On that voyage, in the Columbia Dining Room, I was seated close to two rather grand ladies – they were the mothers of Elizabeth Taylor and Rock Hudson.

I gave many, many talks (beginning in 1980) aboard *QE2*. She had the finest shipboard lecture programme of her time. I once recall Meryl Streep being aboard and she followed me in the ship's theatre. The list of others is very long. And the staff was pure Cunard: the great captains, hotel managers, stewards and restaurant waiters. I recall barman George Coleman, who served aboard Cunard ships for fifty-one years, beginning with the *Berengaria* in 1936. Others dated from the 1940s, and of course so many had served on the earlier Queens – and many had great stories.

In August 1988, I had just returned home (to New Jersey) from Japan. I would be returning to my job, as a middle school teacher in Hoboken, in a week's time. Suddenly, Cunard phoned – could I come to London and join the *QE2*? A film was being made. Well, I half-jokingly responded: 'Well, if you send me on Concorde.' And to my great surprise, they did! I had the unique opportunity to experience that extraordinary aircraft and what was then said to be the last Atlantic liner as well as the last large ocean liner.

I have left out other things, I am sure, but variously I 'launched' several new books in the Ocean Bookshop, had my 50th birthday luncheon in the Princess Grill and was aboard *QE2* for the first tandem crossing, with *QM2*, in April 2004. And, with some sadness, I was aboard *QE2*'s 'Farewell to the British Isles' cruise in October 2008, followed by her final westbound crossing to New York.

Yes, there are many connections; I still miss *QE2*.

WARTIME QUEEN

I am pleased to welcome you back as *QE2*
returns to home waters.

**HM Queen Elizabeth the Queen Mother as *QE2* returned
from the Falklands War**

From as early as the Crimean War, Cunard's fleet has been called upon to serve the Crown in military conflicts. During the First World War, many Cunard liners were requisitioned for wartime use. Perhaps most notably, *Mauretania* and *Aquitania* served as both troop carriers and hospital ships during the conflict. The Second World War saw *QE2*'s predecessors, *Queen Mary* and *Queen Elizabeth*, used extensively for trooping duties. The Queens sailed as far abroad as Australia, operating a high-capacity trooping service, and were acknowledged by Winston Churchill as helping shorten the war by at least a year, due to their troop-carrying ability. They were not alone, with veteran *Aquitania*, the second *Mauretania*, *Georgic*, *Britannic* and many other Cunarders answering the call to defend Great Britain. Many of the past Cunard ships had been built with assistance from government funding, with the understanding that they be created to military specifications to allow them to be used as armed merchant cruisers in the event of war.

QE2's entry into service in 1969 saw her arrive over twenty years after the Second World War, and while government funding had been accessed to build the ship, little consideration had been made regarding her potential alternative use as a troopship. However this was all to change on 3 May 1982 when Captain Alexander Hutcheson heard reports on BBC Radio 2 that his ship was one of a handful requisitioned by the government for use in the Falklands War. The news was subsequently confirmed via official channels, and *QE2* was ordered back to Southampton to commence a mammoth eight-day refurbishment, which would transform the world's best-known cruise ship into a troop carrier.

These works were swift and brutal. The aft end of the Quarter and Upper Decks were sliced off to make way for helipads, allowing *QE2* to carry Sea King helicopters. An additional secondary helipad was created on the ship's bow. The ship's interior was reinforced, with steel plating being laid across the passenger decks, and mess halls were

Above: *QE2* was 'STUFT' – Ship Taken Up From Trade. (Michael Gallagher / Cunard)

Left: Target practice aboard *QE2* – in this case from the Boat Deck, aft. (Commodore R.W. Warwick, *QE2: The Cunard Flagship Queen Elizabeth II*)

Far left: Fuel transfer trials occurred between *QE2* and *Grey Rover*. (Commodore R.W. Warwick, *QE2: The Cunard Flagship Queen Elizabeth II*)

Left: *QE2*'s forward helideck is covered in ice as she sails into the cold water of the South Atlantic. (Commodore R.W. Warwick, *QE2: The Cunard Flagship Queen Elizabeth II*)

Left: A sea king helicopter takes off from *QE2*'s aft helideck. (Commodore R.W. Warwick, *QE2: The Cunard Flagship Queen Elizabeth II*)

Below: *QE2*'s troops are transferred during her call at Cumberland Bay. (Commodore R.W. Warwick, *QE2: The Cunard Flagship Queen Elizabeth II*)

Above: P&O's *Canberra* was also called into service. Here she awaits *QE2*'s arrival in Cumberland Bay. (Commodore R.W. Warwick, *QE2: The Cunard Flagship Queen Elizabeth II*)

created in the Double Down Room. QE2's priceless original artwork was removed from the ship and stored ashore.

On 12 May, the 5th Infantry Brigade, comprising the Scots Guards, Welsh Guards and Gurkhas, embarked aboard QE2: a total of 3,000 troops. The ship sailed that same day, with an emotional farewell to the sound of bagpipes – although a boiler problem meant she wasn't able to make way to deep-ocean until the next day. During the voyage, QE2 was operated by many of her Cunard crew, who volunteered to serve aboard the ship during the dangerous voyage south.

Sending a liner with a name so closely linked to the reigning British monarch was deemed a necessary risk for military planners. QE2 was large enough to carry the required complement of soldiers as well as being a fast liner, meaning she could deliver her complement of troops in a timely manner. However, her reputation meant that her use as a troop ship made international news, so there was no surprise element in her approach. The Argentinian military thus quickly formed plans to target QE2 with its highly effective Exocet missiles. Furthermore, QE2's aluminium superstructure was a concern, as the aluminium was far more susceptible to fire than steel.

To reduce the risk presented to the Cunard flagship, plans were formulated to ensure that QE2 was not in the warzone, with the ship ordered to Cumberland Bay where her troops were transferred to the waiting P&O flagship Canberra for the most dangerous part of the journey. On top of this, the ship's journey to and from the South Atlantic was expedited, with plans formulated to allow QE2 to refuel at sea, thus reducing the time the ship had to remain in dangerous waters. As QE2 was a passenger ship and such an operation was never intended when the ship was designed, a rehearsal was conducted between the outbound QE2 and Royal Fleet Auxiliary vessel Grey Rover in the English Channel. Despite its success, on 18 May QE2 diverted to Freetown in Sierra Leone to take on more fuel, as her supplies were running low. The relative isolation of the West African port, as well as tight security, allowed the ship to refuel and depart before the world's press could report on her position.

The daily routine aboard QE2 changed dramatically during her time as a troop ship. The usual shipboard leisure activities of ballroom dancing, deck quoits and high tea gave way to a strictly managed military lifestyle. Target practice was a regular activity, with guns set up on QE2's aft decks, while flight training was conducted with the small fleet of Sea King helicopters being carried aboard the ship.

Ascension Island, which forms part of the British South Atlantic territory, provided a friendly location for QE2 to replenish her food stores. During her time here, the crew implemented a full 'blackout' policy aboard. Portholes and windows were covered with black plastic in an attempt to make the ship less visible at night.

For the remainder of her journey, the ship's watertight doors were closed as a precaution against any possible attack – and against the danger of ice, given the ship's position in the South Atlantic. Military lookouts were stationed at strategic locations around the ship to identify any outward threats to QE2. Her electronic signature was also reduced, with the ship operating under almost complete electronic silence for the remainder of her journey. This put extra pressure on the navigation crew and officers, but they handled the situation with the utmost professionalism and skill.

On 27 May, just after 7 p.m., QE2 arrived at the rendezvous point in Cumberland Bay in the South Sandwich Islands, where Canberra, Norland and the British Admiralty tug Typhoon were waiting for her. During the night, QE2's troops were transferred to the awaiting P&O flagship. By daybreak the operation was complete, and that morning the Sea King helicopters were transferred to Canberra, which had also been fitted with helipads on her top deck.

On 29 May, QE2 took on survivors from HMS Ardent, HMS Coventry and HMS Antelope, who were to return to Southampton. Time was short, as the Admiralty were particularly concerned for QE2's safety following the Argentine attack on the tanker British Wye only 400 miles from Cumberland Bay. Furthermore, British intelligence had identified that the Argentinian military were using a Boeing 707 jet for reconnaissance in the South Atlantic with the aim of locating both QE2 and Canberra, and as such the decision was made to remove QE2 from the South Atlantic as soon as possible. Thus, at 5.30 p.m. on 29 May, she sailed north towards safety.

Her voyage home was by no means a smooth one, as she encountered severe weather conditions. Strong winds and high

QE2 is met by HMY *Britannia*, with the Queen Mother aboard. (Michael Gallagher / Cunard)

Above: Work is under way in the King George V dry dock to return *QE2* to her pre-war glory. (Commodore R.W. Warwick, *QE2: The Cunard Flagship Queen Elizabeth II*)

Right: *QE2*'s aft decks were restored following her return from the Falklands War. (Michael Gallagher / Cunard)

seas battered the ship for two days and made refuelling at sea impossible, resulting in her fuel supplies running dangerously low. This was a tense and dangerous time for the ship: if she ran out of fuel she would be a sitting duck and an easy target for the Argentinian military. By 2 June the situation had not improved. With only 1,000 tons of fuel remaining, the decision was made to attempt the refuelling operation and the ship rendezvoused with the Royal Fleet Auxiliary vessel *Bayleaf*. A total of 3,800 tons of fuel was successfully loaded aboard *QE2*, – enough for the journey home at a cruising speed of 25 knots.

On 11 June, after a month away, the ship entered the River Solent. The Royal Navy's Commander-in-Chief, Admiral

Newly repainted in a light pebble grey, *QE2* is seen here in New York. (Michael Gallagher / Cunard)

QE2 passes the Statue of Liberty wearing her new colour scheme. (Michael Gallagher / Cunard)

Sir John Fieldhouse, arrived aboard *QE2* by helicopter and addressed the survivors. As *QE2* made her way to her berth in Southampton, she was met by the Royal Yacht *Britannia*. Aboard was HM the Queen Mother, who sent a personalised telegram to Captain Jackson:

> I am pleased to welcome you back as *QE2* returns to home waters after your tour of duty in the South Atlantic. The exploits of your own ship's company and the deeds of valour of those who served in *Antelope*, *Coventry* and *Ardent* have been acclaimed throughout the land and I am proud to add my personal tribute.

When *QE2* tied up alongside she had steamed 14,967 miles during her military career. She remained alongside while the military presence disembarked.

Meanwhile, plans were already under way for a significant refurbishment that would return the liner to her former glory. The refit was undertaken at the King George V dry dock, and was partially funded by the British Government. Cunard opted to use this time to undertake further works of its own to upgrade the ship. A major refurbishment, it aimed to repair and restore the ship's interior and exterior. Works included the removal of the ship's helipads, which left significant damage to her aft decks. The ship's elegant aft profile required extensive rebuilding, while the Quarter Deck and One Deck swimming pools were repaired. Work was also carried out on the aft end of Quarter Deck in preparation for a future planned indoor/outdoor lido area.

Cunard was particularly keen to leverage *QE2*'s post-war standing. Her military service had cemented her reputation in the hearts and minds of the British public, and as such it was felt that forward bookings would benefit from a 'relaunch' of the ship and her services. To signify this, Cunard painted *QE2*'s funnel in its distinctive red and black livery – the first time the ship wore such colours. The hull was also repainted in a pale pebble grey. This light colour made the ship appear somewhat ungainly; it also proved very hard to maintain. Within weeks, the hull was rust-streaked and dirty, prompting Cunard to revert to the traditional federal grey scheme.

QE2 IS STUFT

MAUREEN RYAN
QE2 SOCIAL HOSTESS

I remember so clearly 3 May 1982: a bright, breezy day as *QE2* made her way up the English Channel towards Southampton. We had made the crossing back to the UK after our maiden call to Philadelphia, where *QE2* had taken part in the celebrations marking 300 years since the founding of that great city.

During the voyage we had heard some news of the conflict in the Falklands and rumours that *QE2* might be used, but nothing definite. So, it was very much 'business as usual' that last day of the voyage – passengers attending the last quiz or exercise class, a final stroll along the deck, the goodbyes and exchange of addresses, and as ever, that air of excitement, but also nostalgia, as the halcyon days at sea on the beloved *QE2* were coming to a close and the real world awaited. And for the ship, a time of preparation for her next voyage.

Mid morning I gave a port talk for the passengers continuing in the ship, and as I left the theatre the cruise director called. He had invited one of our guest speakers for a pre-lunch drink in his quarters; could I join them? The speaker in question was the one and only Larry Hagman (taking a break from his role as 'JR' in the long running series *Dallas*), travelling with his lovely wife. I had already done a Q&A interview with Mr Hagman earlier in the voyage and it was lovely to meet them both again. The glasses clinked, conversation flowed and the sun streamed through the porthole – a perfect pre-lunch scene on the legendary *QE2* as a transatlantic voyage came to a close.

And then, it all changed. Suddenly, a knock at the door. It flew open; a staff member stood before us, eyes wide. 'I've just heard, it's on the radio, *QE2* has been requisitioned for the Falklands.' And so it was a reality and our lovely ship, like so many before her, had been called for duty and was STUFT – 'Ship Taken Up from Trade'.

GOING TO BARBADOS

CAPTAIN NICK BATES

It was February 1976, not long after I had passed my master's ticket at the now defunct Leith Nautical College. (Before anyone else does, I should point out that passing my master's ticket with a surname such as mine was something of a two-edged sword.) Anyway, on this particular morning as I was sitting in my small flat in Edinburgh preparing to join my next ship (a bulk carrier in Japan belonging to my then company, Port Line) the phone rang. On the other end was a very well-spoken English gentleman claiming to be the marine superintendent for Cunard Line, the parent company of Port Line. Without much more introduction he explained he was looking for a 'master mariner' to join the famed QE2 in Barbados in five days' time. He went on to explain that my name had been recommended by the marine superintendent from Port Line. Not being quite sure if this was a wind-up from one of my crazy friends, I cautiously declined the kind offer, being sure I was more of a cargo ship sailor than one suited to what was and arguably still is the most famous cruise liner in the world. Rather astutely on his part, he offered to let me think about his offer overnight, saying he would call me back in the morning.

That evening as I walked along the street, in the general direction of my local, a current song of the time kept running through my head. 'Woah, I'm going to Barbados', by a group called Typically Tropical. It was this song that made me think that if the gentleman from Cunard were to call back then I would accept his offer. Sure enough the next morning, the phone rang and after a rather brief conversation I agreed to fly out to Barbados to join QE2 for a two-month contract, after which time I was free to return to Port Line. Four days later I dusted off my best sports coat, put on my smartest shirt, tie and trousers, and boarded the plane to London and then another to Barbados.

The flights themselves passed in something of a blur, partly because of my excitement and partly because I was unaccustomed to long-haul flying. On arrival at Grantley Adams International Airport the door of the plane opened and I was hit by a blast of intense tropical heat. Undaunted, I disembarked and went in search of my luggage. After clearing customs, I hailed one of the many waiting taxis and asked the driver in what was my 'done this a hundred times before' voice to take me to

QE2, explaining quite unnecessarily that it was 'a very big cruise liner'.

Those who know Barbados would be aware that the local transport drops you off at the entrance to the harbour and from there you can take a shuttle bus to your ship should it be docked at the end of the breakwater. Being unaware of the shuttle buses, I proceeded to walk the quarter of a mile or so along the dockside, carrying my two very heavy suitcases – no wheels in those days. On reaching the ship I must have looked like a bit of a wet dish with my best clothes hanging all over while streams of perspiration ran down my face and neck.

As I approached the ship I couldn't help but look up in awe at her stunningly beautiful lines and just the sheer size of her lying alongside the breakwater, secured by several steel mooring wires, the size of which I had never seen before. As I got closer I could see an extremely smart officer sporting an immaculate white uniform standing at the top of the gangway watching line after line of passengers disembark the ship presumably on their way to enjoy the highlights of Barbados. As I approached the gangway the officer asked very politely if he could help me. 'Nice,' I thought, as the sweat continued to pour off my forehead. 'Thank you,' I replied. 'I have come to join the *QE2*.'

'As a passenger or crew?'

'Er, crew,' I responded.

Suddenly his demeanour changed somewhat and, pointing to a spot somewhat away from the bottom of the gangway, told me to 'wait there.' After what seemed like fifteen minutes waiting in the tropical sunshine, he again bellowed, ordering me to 'come here' at the same time enforcing his command with the index finger of his right hand.

'What are you joining as?' he asked.

'Er, second officer, Sir,' I blurted.

Suddenly he sprang to attention, saluted, called me 'sir' and rushed down the gangway to help me on board with my luggage. And so began my two-month contract on board *QE2*, a contract that was to last nearly thirty-five years and ended with my being captain of what was the 'Greatest Ship in the World'.

The ship at sea, following her post-Falklands refurbishment. (Michael Gallagher / Cunard)

eight

THE TRANSPLANT

Tomorrow's Superliner, Today.

Cunard describes *QE2*'s 1986–87 refit

The early 1980s were difficult times for *QE2*. New issues with her steam turbine engines began to develop, resulting in numerous breakdowns and a reduction in reliability. When *QE2* was designed, a degree of redundancy was planned for her power plant. However, budget constraints due to Cunard's deteriorating financial position in the 1960s resulted in much of the redundancy being removed, leaving the Cunard flagship with the minimum number of turbines to achieve her top cruising speed. While this saved Cunard money at the outset, it meant that any issue with one of the ship's three turbines could significantly affect her service speed and thus the timeliness of her schedule.

In 1983, the ship was sent to the Lloyd Werft shipyard in Bremerhaven, Germany. Here, work was undertaken on the aft of Quarter Deck. A sliding glass roof (known as a magrodome) was installed over the swimming pool, creating an indoor/outdoor area. This allowed the Lido restaurant to be extended aft under the newly covered space, while ensuring the pool could be used in all weather conditions.

Over the next two years, *QE2*'s reliability continued to concern Cunard. The company decided to investigate options for a permanent solution – replacing *QE2*'s engines or the more extreme action of replacing the ship with a new liner. Building a new transatlantic liner to the size and scale of *QE2* proved cost-prohibitive. Despite the US $75 million price tag, re-engining the ship was deemed an acceptable alternative. A state-of-the-art diesel electric power plant was selected to power the ship, with MAN B&W chosen to provide the engines. The diesels would power two gigantic British-built GEC propulsion motors. Cunard awarded the refurbishment contract to Lloyd Werft. The shipyard already had experience working on *QE2*, and preliminary work was commenced ahead of the ship's arrival.

Despite the mechanical issues facing her, *QE2* was still able to make headlines. One such occurrence took place in May 1985 when, while at sea, *QE2* was overflown by Concorde and the Red Arrows. The perfectly orchestrated event saw the aircraft, flying in a V formation, pass over *QE2*, which was at sea under full steam. The resulting photo was widely publicised.

On 20 October 1986, *QE2* departed New York for the final time under steam power. The subsequent transatlantic crossing was the last in a 146-year tradition of Cunard steamship crossings. By the time *QE2* arrived at Bremerhaven on 27 October and the engines were powered down, she had steamed over 2.6 million miles. Here, an army of workers commenced what was the largest marine conversion yet attempted. Over 4,700 tons of old machinery had to be removed from *QE2*'s lower decks. Cunard was not willing to risk any damage to *QE2*'s hull, and as

Left: *QE2* completed the final Cunard steam crossing in 1986. (Michael Gallagher / Cunard)

Below: The aft profile of *QE2* was altered with the addition of the magrodome above the Quarter Deck pool. It is seen here in the open position. (Michael Gallagher / Cunard)

such cutting a hole in the ship's side to remove the scrap metal was out of the question. Instead the ship's original funnel was removed, opening up the shaft that ran from the funnel to the engine room. From here, the old power plant was craned out, while the new engines were lowered in the same way.

Cunard opted to power *QE2* with nine medium-speed MAN B&W diesel electric engines. Each engine had an output of 10,620kW and weighed 220 tons. The nine engines offered the ship an excellent level of redundancy, with three required to maintain hotel services and up to nine when travelling at a top speed of 32.5 knots. The diesel plant was arranged into the forward and aft engine room, to best utilise the space made available by the removed steam plant. Each engine operated at 440rpm and generated electricity, which was then fed to various areas of the ship. Some of the electricity was used to power hotel services – everything from lights to air conditioning.

A large percentage of the electricity generated by the plant was fed into the ship's two propulsion motors. Built by GEC of England, in 1986 they were the largest single-unit propulsion motors ever built for a commercial vessel, weighing an impressive 295 tons apiece. About the size of two double-decker buses, they were rated at 44mW. The motors were used to drive two new propeller shafts, which in turn drove two five-bladed variable-pitch propellers. The propeller shaft operated at 144rpm when *QE2* was at sea, with the pitch of the propeller used to determine the speed at which the vessel operated. Furthermore, this could be reduced to 72rpm during berthing procedures. Interestingly, *QE2*'s new power plant had no traditional 'reverse' function, with the ship's direction also controlled by the propeller pitch.

Above: Workers cut up scrap metal in the shadow of the funnel. Over 4,700 tons of scrap was removed from *QE2* during her re-engining in 1986–87. (Michael Gallagher / Cunard)

Left: One of the huge propulsion motors is craned aboard the ship. (Michael Gallagher / Cunard)

Left: The funnel-less *QE2* during her re-engining refurbishment. (Michael Gallagher / Cunard)

Bottom left: Workers built a roof over the top of *QE2*'s aft decks to protect them from the cold weather – note the ice on the water. (Michael Gallagher / Cunard)

Bottom right: Inside *QE2*'s engine room during the refit. (Michael Gallagher / Cunard)

Top left: The new funnel was built on the dockside. (Michael Gallagher / Cunard)

Left: The ship is ready to receive her new funnel. (Michael Gallagher / Cunard)

Above: The new funnel is craned out of the warehouse. (Michael Gallagher / Cunard)

Left: *QE2* receives her new, fatter funnel. (Michael Gallagher / Cunard)

Below left and right: The ship with new funnel attached. (Michael Gallagher / Cunard)

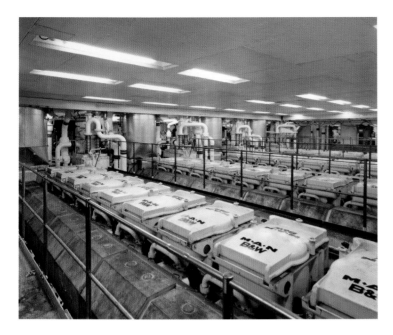

Above: One of the two completed diesel engine rooms. (Michael Gallagher / Cunard)

Right top and bottom: The ship undergoing trials following her re-engining. (Michael Gallagher / Cunard)

With the installation of the new machinery, the vessel now had nine large exhaust pipes to accommodate. This increased ventilation required the original funnel to be remodelled, resulting in a new, thicker funnel that dramatically altered the ship's exterior profile. This was coupled with further exterior alterations: eight new balcony suites were built on Signal Deck, straightening *QE2*'s top profile and adding valuable revenue-generating space to the ship.

The ship's interior was also altered. In the Double Down Room twin staircases were built at the forward end and a new 'starlight' ceiling created. The shopping promenade on Boat Deck was reworked, with the addition of a variety of designer labels including Christian Dior and Cartier. Forward on Upper Deck, the Tables of the World restaurant was reworked into the Mauretania, taking its name from Cunard's record-breaker of 1907, while the Midships Lobby was given white leather seating.

When *QE2* sailed on her sea trials, the new power plant exceeded expectations. The ship bested her steam speed record, with a top recorded speed of just under 34 knots. Furthermore, she was more economical than before: an important result for Cunard.

Despite 1.7 million man-hours being consumed during the refurbishment, *QE2* was not fully complete when handed back to Cunard. As such, workers stayed to tidy up outstanding issues in an unsuccessful attempt to complete the ship before she arrived in Southampton.

THE HERITAGE TRAIL

THOMAS QUINONES

QE2 CRUISE STAFF

QE2 sailed her final voyage to the waters of Dubai back in November 2008, and in 2012, after more than thirty years, I left Cunard service for life ashore. Some eight years later, I still find snapshots of *QE2*'s Heritage Trail and comments posted by viewers on the Internet. Although memories of this apparently legendary institution continue to live on in electronic form, they are somewhat two-dimensional, lacking the essential spark of the full, unabated live performance. As is commonly quoted about many events in life, 'you just had to be there' to appreciate the bigger picture, which was given depth and texture by those personal feelings and emotions experienced at that particular point in time.

In its simplest form, heritage in the forms of art, artefacts and history was always present for all of those who cared to see, pause and take a closer look. Daily shipboard routine would sweep you past various pieces of an extensive and eclectic collection but not in any particular order, logical or chronological context. For many passengers, there was always somewhere to go, something to do. Heritage was just part of the ship's decor, fixtures and fittings encountered on the way to wherever.

So how did Thomas Quinones, with a half Puerto Rican, half German heritage of his own, bring presentation of the history of the British Cunard Line, aboard its flagship, to life and give it a style all its own for which it is still remembered? I will tell you. To quote: 'Fasten your seatbelts. It's going to be a bumpy ride!'

Presentation of simple facts and figures, although informative, is undoubtedly dull for anyone other than dedicated buffs of the subject in question and will not hold an audience captive for long. What is needed is more than a bit of theatrical flair and the personality to carry it off. To this already heady mix, add a voice of character and unique expression. Rising up from two decks below, then spilling out from the head of D Stairway comes enthusiastic commentary on the painting of 'Queen Elizabeth, our dear Queen Mother … indeed.' Those unmistakeable tones remain clearly audible as far aft along Boat Deck as the balcony of the Grand Lounge. Add costume, colour, context and the forty-five-minute daily programme slots allocated for the Heritage Trail, and you have an epic production of all consuming entertainment, that had been known to last for anything up to three hours with the audience remaining largely intact. Who needs lunch or afternoon tea?

History depicted within monochrome murals located within the Midships Lobby, barely given a second glance by passengers caught up in the pandemonium and distractions of embarkation or disembarkation, comes to life once the ship is at sea and it is explained animatedly by a man dressed in formal top hat and tails. He makes his sudden and unexpected entrance to the accompaniment of the swish of a red velvet curtain and transports you back in time to the very beginnings of the company in 1840. My transformation into character is complete, that familiar chill runs down my spine. The gasps of awe from the audience tell me that they are hooked. The journey through time is under way.

Stage port: a group of ladies, attired in Victorian finery, enter and pass by on their daily promenade, chatting with each other as they go. Stage Starboard: Time rolls on. Diamonds, furs, cigarette holders! Enter the stars of Hollywood portraying the glamour and sophistication of the golden age of ocean liner travel. Captivated, the gathered throng ascends the stairs up to Quarter Deck. Here, a peek into the first-class domain of the floating palaces, *Mauretania*, *Aquitania* and *Berengaria*. Characters dressed for the evening are gathered at a table set with crisp white linen. They sip champagne by candlelight as dancers swirl by. A Viennese waltz plays vividly in the imagination.

Exit the dancers and enter all into the Chartroom. The mood is darker, sombre. The world is at war. A lone serviceman representing the many thousands of troops transported aboard the Cunard Queens stands beside the art deco piano from *Queen Mary*. He sings soulfully for home and longed for reunion with loved ones. Emotions are stirred, heart strings stretched to breaking point. The tears well in many an eye. It's raw, indelibly raw.

Traditionally, the Heritage Trail concluded on Upper Deck with the Boston Commemorative Cup. However, times were changing. *QE2* having achieved the status of Grand Dame of the Cunard fleet, surpassing the service record set previously by *Aquitania*, was to be retired.

New Queens, *Mary 2* and *Victoria*, were already at sea gathering followers of their own and another *Elizabeth* – of this, rather than the last, century – was set to follow. A new generation expresses different attitudes, different lifestyles, and different values. The Heritage Trail had to adapt to reflect these changes too. The final performances signed off with a forward-looking tribute and symbolic handover to these 'new kids on the block'.

From stage aft: enter the youngsters, lining up outside the entrance doors of the Yacht Club. Bold, modern, fashionable, they wave their Union flags in salute to Cunard past, present and future. The curtain falls, another performance ends and I'm back in the real world. I'm drained both physically and emotionally. Questions from the audience follow.

Frequently asked is: 'How do you manage to do that?' Information and all those facts came to me so naturally, everything right at hand, as if gained through personal experience. I have always felt an affinity with a bygone age. Could it be that I had another existence at sea prior to this one? Delivery was almost effortless; the words simply flowed out of my mouth as if someone was placing them there. Maybe a spirit from the past – perhaps even Sir Samuel Cunard himself? The answer, 'I don't know,' still stands to this day. One cannot explain the unexplainable. After all, is it not the element of mystery that is responsible for the creation and endurance of legends?

nine

BACK TO WORK

QE2 LOVES NY.

A large banner hung from *QE2*'s boat deck when
she arrived in New York Harbor after
her 'second maiden voyage'

The newly re-engined *QE2* was handed back to Cunard on 25 April 1987 and after a few days alongside in Southampton she was reintroduced into Cunard service on 27 April. The ship's first commercial voyage under diesel power was a charity event hosted by HRH Princess Diana, who escorted a group of underprivileged school children aboard. *QE2* made the short passage to the Isle of Wight, before returning to the quay at Southampton in preparation for her journey to New York.

Dubbed the 'second maiden voyage', this crossing was heralded as the official rebirth of the world's most famous ship. However, a change in British maritime law meant Cunard no longer had to maintain a British crew aboard *QE2*. As such, there were many new crew aboard the ship for this trip and, while the voyage was heavily booked, the new crew's inexperience was noticed by regular passengers.

When *QE2* arrived in New York she received an enthusiastic welcome. *QE2* visited New York more than any other port except Southampton. She was a familiar sight in the city and many New Yorkers travelled aboard. Prior to docking, a large banner reading '*QE2* LOVES NY' was draped over the ship's side to pay homage to this connection.

Part of *QE2*'s re-engining work had been the installation of a new set of five-bladed propellers. These were initially designed to work in tandem with two sets of Grim wheels. These wheels

The updated and refreshed Columbia restaurant. Note the Boston (Britannia) Cup, visible. (Michael Gallagher / Cunard)

Above left: The 1987 incarnation of the Yacht Club complete with custom-built piano bar. (Michael Gallagher / Cunard)

Above: Although largely unchanged, the Queens Room received new furniture. (Michael Gallagher / Cunard)

Left: The updated Shopping Promenade featured brand-name outlets. (Michael Gallagher / Cunard)

Above: Tables of the World became Mauretania restaurant in the 1986–87 refit. (Michael Gallagher / Cunard)

Above right: The original Grill Room, reborn as Princess Grill (Port). (Michael Gallagher / Cunard)

were set aft of the propellers and connected to a separate internal propeller shaft. They were designed to capture some of the lost energy from the propeller wash to drive a small turbine, thus reducing fuel consumption. While ingenious in design, they proved unsuccessful in practice, with several blades snapping off. They also created a vibration issue aboard the ship that caused discomfort for passengers and crew alike. In 1988, following *QE2*'s first world voyage as a diesel ship, the issue was addressed with the ship returning to Bremerhaven. Here two sets of new 6.1m-diameter propellers were installed and the vibration issue was resolved. The Grim wheels were subsequently removed from *QE2* and the space capped off.

Despite her brief return to Bremerhaven and the 1987 stock market crash, which had affected cruise bookings, *QE2*'s early years as a diesel-powered liner were a resounding success.

Key events included participation in Australia's bicentennial celebrations. The ship hosted a gala ball while alongside in Sydney Harbour, with Australia's then-Prime Minister Bob Hawke in attendance.

In December 1988, *QE2* hosted a special event to celebrate the 50th anniversary of the launch of RMS *Queen Elizabeth*. To commemorate this anniversary, HM Queen Elizabeth the Queen Mother, who had named *Queen Elizabeth* in 1938, boarded *QE2*. Following a tour of the ship, she addressed attendees in the Columbia (later Caronia) restaurant before being presented with a silver model of *Queen Elizabeth*.

With *QE2*'s reputation soaring, the liner was given a boost in 1989 when she was chartered twice for use as a hotel ship in Japan. This was particularly pleasing for Cunard, as the continuing effects of the 1987 crash meant that these charters were more profitable for the company than under booked cruises. The first charter took place in March and coincided with the 130th anniversary of Yokohama, while the second occurred between December 1989 and May 1990, when *QE2* was used as a floating hotel in Osaka during the World Exposition. The latter charter meant *QE2* was not available to undertake her annual world cruise, and as such Cunard used *Vistafjord* for the 107-day voyage in 1990. Following her time in

Osaka, *QE2* embarked on a series of cruises in the South China Sea and Pacific Ocean, her popularity soaring in the region. The success of *QE2*'s Asian itineraries led many to believe the ship would undertake regular Asian cruises.

In 1990, *QE2* completed her fastest ever transatlantic crossing. Under the command of Captain Robin Woodall, the vessel completed the transit in four days, six hours and fifty-seven minutes at an impressive average speed of 30 knots. It was also a year of celebration, with Cunard's 150th anniversary occurring that July. To mark the occasion, *QE2* was sent to Liverpool for the first time in her career. Here, over 1 million people lined the banks of the River Mersey to see the ship, which anchored near the Cunard Building. Other special calls during the 150th celebrations included *QE2* returning to Greenock – her first visit since entering service – as well as a maiden call at Cobh, Ireland.

In 1992 the ship made headlines for all the wrong reasons when, during an August cruise up the east coast of the United States, she ran aground on the southern tip of Sow and Pigs Reef, off Martha's Vineyard. Sailing under the command of Captain Woodall and with a pilot aboard, *QE2* was enjoying an otherwise uneventful journey when a number of noticeable vibrations alerted those on the Bridge that something had gone awry. With the ship stopped, watertight doors closed and crew called to muster stations, the Bridge officers went about inspecting the damage. This survey revealed that her double bottom had been breached. With *QE2* taking on water, calculations were made to assess the stability of the ship. Fortunately it was discovered she was structurally sound. The United States Coast Guard was alerted and oil containment buoys were set up to protect the local environment. The resulting investigation found that the charts in the region were half a century out of date and recorded the depth of the water incorrectly. *QE2* sailed for Newport where her passengers were disembarked.

Above left: The Quarter Deck pool under the glass magrodome. (Michael Gallagher / Cunard)

Left: The Double Down Room was recreated as the Grand Lounge. (Michael Gallagher / Cunard)

Right: Princess Diana with Captain Lawrence Portet during a concert in the Grand Lounge, 1987. (Michael Gallagher / Cunard)

Below: The newly re-engined *QE2* at sea. (Michael Gallagher / Cunard)

During various 1980s refits, *QE2*'s aft decks were dramatically changed with the addition of the magrodome and the alpha and beta tenders, and the new interior spaces on Boat Deck. (Michael Gallagher / Cunard)

Queen Elizabeth 2
SOUTHAMPTON

Above left: The ship passes the White Cliffs of Dover. (Michael Gallagher / Cunard)

Above: An aerial view of *QE2* in the late 1980s shows the completed Signal Deck balcony suites. (Michael Gallagher / Cunard)

Left: The *QE2* in Sydney, Australia, during a world cruise. (Michael Gallagher / Cunard)

Speeding through the ocean. *QE2* was the fastest passenger ship in service for much of her career. (Michael Gallagher / Cunard)

Above: *QE2* takes on a pilot during a departure. (Michael Gallagher / Cunard)

Right: HM the Queen Mother gave a speech in the Columbia restaurant to celebrate fifty years since the launch of RMS *Queen Elizabeth* in 1988. (Michael Gallagher / Cunard)

The ship then proceeded to Boston where she was dry docked. The subsequent inspection revealed significant damage to the hull, requiring precision work with a high grade of steel that the Boston yard was unable to accommodate. Temporary repairs were made to *QE2* to allow her to complete a transatlantic crossing to Germany, where she was received at the Blohm + Voss shipyard in Hamburg. Here, she was dry docked once more and permanent repairs were made to the hull. The repair work was a significant job, and this plus the time

lost in the failed Boston attempt meant Cunard had to cancel several of *QE2*'s voyages.

QE2 was never far from the spotlight and was often the subject of television coverage. One such occasion occurred in 1993, when an episode of the popular British sitcom *Keeping Up Appearances* was filmed aboard *QE2*. The event saw the cast of the TV show sail aboard the ship, which was operating a regular passenger voyage. Several members of the ship's company were enlisted to appear on screen, with Captain (later

Commodore) John Burton-Hall and First Officer (later Captain) Ian McNaught appearing in the episode. The script allowed lead character Hyacinth Bucket (played by Patricia Routledge) to explore the ship, showing many public rooms on screen, including the Queens Room, Lido, Boardroom, Grand Lounge, Theatre, and a One Deck cabin. While it offered excellent publicity for Cunard, the footage reveals how mismatched and confused QE2's interior had become. QE2 had been a vibrant, modern and trendy floating resort when she was first put into service in the late 1960s. But in addition to the original designs now being dated, a variety of refurbishments over the years had added a kaleidoscope of styles to her once coherent interior. Something had to be done to restore QE2's internal identity and make the ship relevant for the twenty-first century.

HM the Queen is presented with a token of her visit to QE2 by Sir Nigel Broackes of Trafalgar House in 1990. (Michael Gallagher / Cunard)

Above left: *QE2* and HMY *Britannia* together during the 'Royal Review' in Southampton, 1990. (Michael Gallagher / Cunard)

Left: *QE2* near the Cunard Building where she was designed, 1990. (Michael Gallagher / Cunard)

Above: Captain Robin Woodall and former British Prime Minister Margaret Thatcher during her Falklands War 10th anniversary visit. (Michael Gallagher / Cunard)

Tour Guide

ACCOMMODATION DECKS

Signal Deck

The highest deck aboard *QE2*, Signal Deck was the location of the Bridge. This was *QE2*'s command centre and the place where primary navigation was undertaken. Nicknamed 'The Tank' by the officers and crew (due to its small size), the Bridge was set forward of Signal Deck and offers an unobstructed view forward over the bow.

Unlike the enclosed, sheltered Bridge wings of modern cruise ships, *QE2*'s were open to the elements. Decked in teak wood, they sported a classic appearance, with swept-back lines that evoked a traditional ocean liner. However, they were not there for aesthetic reasons; the Bridge wings formed the critical function of offering the captain and Bridge crew excellent sightlines during manoeuvring and docking procedures. To suit this purpose, they extended over each side of *QE2* and included a waterproof console that mirrored the main driving equipment for steering, bow thrusters, speed and the whistle.

Aft of the Bridge, but still enclosed within the Bridge structure, was *QE2*'s chartroom. This space housed the paper charts, which covered all areas of the world. While *QE2*'s navigation was computerised in her latter years, paper charts were maintained throughout the ship's career.

Before 9/11, it was possible to tour *QE2*'s Bridge, with specially arranged groups escorted through the area by one of the ship's senior officers. The tour covered all aspects of operating the ship, including the opportunity to hold *QE2*'s wheel.

Further aft, Signal Deck was home to a series of penthouse suites. These suites were all added to *QE2* after the ship entered service, with the first block added in 1972, followed by two subsequent additions in 1977 and 1986–87. There were thirty-two balcony suites, the best of these being the multi-level Queen Elizabeth and Queen Mary penthouses. The largest accommodation aboard the ship, these penthouses featured a forward facing balcony, dining room, bedroom and separate lounge area. There was a balcony overlooking the Boat Deck as well as a separate balcony and conservatory facing forward, which overlooked the Bridge.

Top: *QE2*'s port Bridge wing and teak-wood deck. (Frame / Cross)

Centre and bottom: The Queen Elizabeth Suite was one of the two grandest suites aboard *QE2*. (Michael Gallagher / Cunard)

Behind the suites, you would find the ship's 21.2m (69ft 6in) funnel, the second that *QE2* has carried; it was rebuilt in 1986–87 during the ship's conversion from steam to diesel propulsion. The original funnel was much thinner than the current one, and its replacement with a thicker funnel gave *QE2* a bolder, more commanding profile. Interestingly, several panels of the original funnel were used to create the new funnel.

QE2 carried more than 2.5 million human passengers during her service career; however, what is often less well known is that the ship was one of the few vessels in service that could also carry dogs and cats. The ship's kennels were located on Signal Deck and accessed from a stairway off Sun Deck. They came complete with a 'doggy deck' near the base of the funnel. This space included a London lamppost and a New York fire hydrant – for the dogs' convenience.

Sun Deck

Originally named Sports Deck, this deck was the second highest aboard *QE2* and housed a sheltered, open-air sporting deck with tennis courts and deck quoits for first-class passengers. Largely rebuilt when the suites were added in 1972, the deck was devoid of sporting facilities for most of *QE2*'s career. The deck was eventually renamed Sun Deck in 1994, by which time there hadn't been any sporting facilities on the deck for twenty-two years.

At the very forward end of Sun Deck, accessible via staircases from Boat Deck, was the Observation Deck. Fondly nicknamed the 'bit beneath the Bridge' by *QE2* regulars, it spanned the full width of the ship and was the only passenger area that offered a forward view, as the original observation lounge had been removed in 1972.

Just behind the Observation Deck was the Captain's Cabin. Situated just under the Bridge, it offered easy access for the captain to the command centre and retained much of its original character during *QE2*'s long career. On rare occasions, select passengers would be invited to private cocktail functions in this exclusive part of the ship.

Sun Deck housed twelve Queens Grill suites. Of these, ten included balconies, while two were large ocean-view staterooms. Each of *QE2*'s penthouse suites on both Signal and Sun Decks, along with the deluxe cabins built on Boat Deck, were numbered in the 8000 range, utilising cabin numbers not already used by *QE2*'s existing passenger accommodation. Aft of the suites, Sun Deck housed a children's nursery. Here, professionally trained nannies were available to look after children, while the space also offered a night-care service. This allowed travelling

Below: *QE2*'s forward observation platform. (Frame / Cross)

Below right: The Sun Deck area aft of Funnel Bar. (Frame / Cross)

parents to enjoy the ship's nightlife, secure in the knowledge that their children were being well cared for. *QE2*'s senior officers' accommodation was also found on Sun Deck.

At the aft end of Sun Deck was a large teak-wood sheltered deck. First-class passengers used this area for sunbathing when *QE2* first entered service, and deck-chairs could be reserved in advance from the dedicated deck steward. Once *QE2* was converted into a classless ship, the deck was available for all passengers.

The aft deck area also doubled as a helicopter deck, allowing for helicopters to land aboard *QE2*. The aluminium deck plating in this area was thickened, allowing small- to medium-sized helicopters to land aboard the ship. This occurred on several occasions, including during Cunard's 150th anniversary in 1990, when Sir Nigel Broakes, chairman of Trafalgar House (then the owner of Cunard), arrived by helicopter.

Throughout much of *QE2*'s career, the deck was largely underutilised. As such, when *QE2* was moved into a permanent cruising role in 2004, a new establishment called Funnel Bar was built at the base of the funnel. The works included the addition of shade sails and teak-wood tables, and greatly improved the usability of this space.

The penthouse corridor on Sun Deck. (Frame / Cross)

One Deck

From a passenger perspective, One Deck was one of the shorter decks aboard *QE2*. However this was an illusion, as One Deck was actually the longest deck aboard the ship, spanning a full 963ft. The forward third of the deck was utilised by crew areas, meaning passengers couldn't fully appreciate the length of this deck. Crew-only areas included the anchor housing, crew accommodation, a crew mess and crew office.

Passenger accommodation was housed on this deck, beginning just forward of the D Stairway landing. Originally housing first-class accommodation, One Deck was home to Grill- and Caronia-grade accommodation by the time *QE2* retired. Prior to the installation of the Signal and Sun Deck balcony cabins, the largest and best-appointed cabins were found on this deck, including suites with large picture windows. The majority of cabins on One Deck had multiple portholes, while some of the smaller Caronia-grade cabins had single portholes. One Deck also housed eight inside cabins.

Between 1984 and 1996, One Deck housed the only seagoing branch of Harrods. This shop was originally decorated in a unique colour scheme of gold and green, to reflect the distinctive Harrods brand, and remained in operation until 1996, when Harrods left the ship. A new store opened on Boat Deck in 1999.

One Deck was also home to the Princess Grill Lounge. Located on C Stairway and accessible from the port side only, the lounge remained virtually untouched throughout most of *QE2*'s career. Decorated in dark maroon leather offset by chrome finishes, the lounge served as a pre-dinner drinks area for passengers who dined in the exclusive Grill restaurant, later renamed the Princess Grill. Following the 1994 refit, and the addition of the Crystal Bar, which also provided access to the restaurant from Upper Deck, the Princess Grill Lounge was not included on *QE2*'s deck plans. Nevertheless, this champagne bar remained open for the duration of the ship's career and was popular with those regular travellers who had discovered its location.

For those seeking extra pampering, cosmetic assistance or just a haircut, the beauty salon and barber's shop was located on One Deck. Accessible off G Stairway, for much of *QE2*'s career it was managed by Steiner's of London.

Much of the remainder of One Deck was dedicated to passenger cabins, with a variety of shapes and sizes available. Cabins included Q-, P- and C-class accommodation and were numbered 1001 to 1121.

At the aft end of One Deck was the Pavilion. Added during the 1994 refit, this casual grill-style eatery offered burgers, hot dogs, chips, salads and a 24/7 ice cream machine, which saw heavy use. This restaurant led out to the One Deck pool. Originally one of *QE2*'s two outdoor pools, the One Deck pool was retained in the 1994 refit and enhanced with the addition of a children's paddling pool area and two Jacuzzis.

Above left: A view along the ship's foredeck. This area housed one of the whistles and anchor casing. It was designated 'crew only'. (Frame / Cross)

Left: The Princess Grill Lounge. (Frame / Cross)

Two Deck

Most passengers who boarded *QE2* during her thirty-nine-and-a-half-year career entered the ship on Two Deck. There were three lobbies on this deck: the Forward Lobby, Midships Lobby and Aft Lobby. The Midships Lobby was by far the most significant of these. When *QE2* entered service, this room was one of the most dramatic changes from the original Queens. Gone were the great art deco reception rooms, replaced by a modern circular design. There was a central, sunken lounge, with seating finished in green leather. Black-clad walls were juxtaposed with chrome finishings, while a central 'trumpet' column supported a ceiling of white rings and mirrors. The room was updated during *QE2*'s service life, with the green leather seating being replaced by white leather, while planter boxes were fitted to the base of the 'trumpet' column. During 1992 and again during the 1994 refurbishment, this space was given a significant overhaul. In keeping with the updated interiors throughout *QE2*, Cunard

Below: The Aquitania Suite was created in 1999 from the space previously housing the Hotel Manager's suite. (Michael Gallagher / Cunard)

HERITAGE
TRAIL

SILVER QE2 MODEL TWO DECK

At the aft end of the Midships Lobby, a silver model of *QE2* was on display in a special glass cabinet, complete with illuminated base plate. Created by Asprey of Bond Street in 1977, the model only joined *QE2*'s Heritage Trail collection in 1999, owing to its whereabouts being something of a mystery for much of its existence. It now resides aboard MV *Queen Elizabeth*. (Frame / Cross)

SPIRIT OF THE ATLANTIC TWO DECK

This bronze statue was designed by Barney Seale. It was commissioned for display aboard the second *Mauretania*. It depicts a naked female form with one hand holding a large bird. It was displayed on Two Deck near the forward exit of the Midships Lobby. (Frame / Cross)

heritage was introduced here in 1994. While the general shape and arrangement of the room was retained, the redesigned decor gave a vastly different first impression. Four large murals were installed depicting various periods of Cunard's history. These included Sir Samuel Cunard and the first Cunarders, the era of the Ocean Greyhounds *Lusitania* and *Mauretania*, the original Queens and the history of *QE2*.

The forward lobby was located off A Stairway, and acted as an embarkation point, a meeting area and a lobby for the popular Computer Learning Centre. This centre was installed aboard *QE2* when computers were a novel and interesting pastime; it

Left: The Midships Lobby, pictured here in 1987, featured dark walls and white leather seating. (Michael Gallagher / Cunard)

Below: The updated lobby as it appeared in early 2008. It was greatly rebuilt during the 1994 refit. (Frame / Cross)

remained until the ship retired, as its function was adapted to become an internet centre, offering access to satellite internet and to printers, as well as classes on how to surf the web.

The aft lobby was located off G Stairway and acted as an embarkation and disembarkation point. This led into passenger corridors that accessed cabins numbered 2001 to 2152, which included two penthouse suites: 2149 Aquitania and 2151 Carinthia.

Another key focal point on Two Deck was the Pursers' Office, Business Centre and Bureau de Change. This area, off F Stairway, was a hub of activity, and was fully refurbished and rebuilt during the 1999 refit. The final layout combined the pursers' function with the money exchange behind an elegantly curved granite desk. Aft of the Pursers' Office was the Business Centre, which offered those working at sea access to the internet, printers and satellite telecommunications.

HERITAGE
TRAIL

FALKLANDS PLAQUE
TWO DECK

Presented to *QE2* by First Sea Lord, Sir John Fieldhouse, in honour of *QE2*'s service in the Falklands campaign, The Falklands Plaque was found on Two Deck at the Forward Lobby, starboard. (Frame / Cross)

QE2'S BELL
THREE DECK

Towards the end of *QE2*'s career,
the ship's bell was situated on the
D Stairway landing of Three Deck. Made
of brass, it was used (upside down) for
christenings as well as for 'ringing in
the New Year'. It now resides aboard
MV *Queen Elizabeth*. (Frame / Cross)

Three Deck

Although One Deck was physically the longest deck aboard *QE2*, from a passenger perspective Three Deck seemed longer, as it had the longest passenger corridor.

The construction of *QE2* differs from modern cruise ships. While today's liners are built in a series of prefabricated blocks, *QE2* was constructed *in situ* on the slipway. As a result, like many of her predecessors the ship has a noticeable sheer. This was visible on Three Deck, as passengers standing at the aft end of the deck wouldn't be able to see the end of the deck, as it sheered upwards as it progressed; the same perspective was observed by those standing at the forward end looking aft.

Cabins numbered 3001 to 3188 were found here, while at the aft end of the deck passengers could access a greenery (florist) and large laundrette. The laundrette had a separate washer/dryer section, as well as an ironing room.

A unique feature of *QE2*, particularly when compared to modern cruise ships, was the inclusion of a Synagogue aboard the ship. Located on Three Deck near A Stairway, this was a peaceful and quiet room designed to allow Jewish passengers to observe their faith. The Synagogue remained virtually untouched between 1969 and 2008. However, a few weeks before *QE2* sailed on her final voyage to Dubai, the religious elements of the room were removed.

A C-grade cabin on Three Deck in a blue theme, in 2008. (Frame / Cross)

Four Deck and Five Deck

Four and Five Deck were the domain of passenger cabins, with Four Deck numbered 4001 to 4266 and Five Deck 5001 through 5243. While passenger areas of Four Deck spanned from forward of A Stairway to aft of H Stairway, from the mid 1990s the aft section of Five Deck was allocated to crew. As such, passenger access was not available past G Stairway. The corridors on Four and Five Decks were treated to an extensive facelift during the 1999 refit, which saw faux-wood veneer panelling and handrails installed, as well as subtle mood lighting in the ceilings.

When *QE2* first came into service, she offered a car transportation service between Europe and America, with entry points to the ship's car-lift on both Four and Five Decks. Observant passengers would notice two areas on the passenger corridor where the carpet gave way to a more industrial floor covering, indicating the locations of the vehicle embarkation points.

When *QE2* was manoeuvring close to shore, such as arriving and departing from port, the lower watertight doors would be closed. As such, passengers on Five Deck could often find their path blocked by large blue (later repainted yellow) doors. However, there were always alternative access points to and from the cabins.

Above: During the 1994 refit, almost all of *QE2*'s bathrooms were updated with art deco-style units. (Frame / Cross)

Left: An inside Mauretania-grade cabin on Five Deck. (Frame / Cross)

ten

REBIRTH

I think you are very brave to be going to sea
this week.

**Prince Andrew after touring *QE2* following the
Project Lifestyle refit**

The future of *QE2*'s interior style was placed in the hands of the British MET Studio under the code name Project Lifestyle. The brief was to create a sense of place aboard *QE2*, improve the passenger flow and enhance both her public spaces and passenger accommodation to keep the ship best-in-class for the remainder of her service career. An impressive £45 million was allocated to the project, which would touch almost every part of the ship's passenger spaces and cabins. Features of the refurbishment included the creation of a new indoor Lido as well as the removal of the unpopular magrodome roof. It also allowed for the reorganisation of *QE2*'s two largest restaurants, the redecoration of all of the ship's major bars and lounges, a reworked show lounge and the rebuilding of every cabin bathroom, replacing the dated fittings with smart, art deco-style units.

The Blohm + Voss shipyard in Hamburg was selected to carry out the work and a very ambitious thirty-two-day schedule was agreed upon. *QE2* arrived in Hamburg on 20 November 1994. The yard employed 2,000 skilled workers, and an additional 400 *QE2* crew stayed with the ship to assist with the refit.

While work commenced on the interior fit out, structural works were being completed to Quarter Deck, aft. Here, the glass magrodome roof was removed and replaced with a teak-wood deck, giving the ship an additional 464sq.m (5,000sq.ft) of deck space. Interior alterations resulted in the passenger flow improving around *QE2*, going back to the

The updated Queens Grill restaurant. (Michael Gallagher / Cunard)

The Queens Grill Lounge prior to the 1994 refit. (Michael Gallagher / Cunard)

Above left: The new Bookshop replaced *QE2*'s Cardroom. (Michael Gallagher / Cunard)

Above: The Golden Lion Pub on Upper Deck replaced the Theatre Bar. (Michael Gallagher / Cunard)

Left: A large model of *Mauretania* on Quarter Deck formed part of the new Heritage Trail. (Michael Gallagher / Cunard)

Below left: The remodelled Grand Lounge. (Michael Gallagher / Cunard)

original design principles of meals and food service forward, lounges amidships and entertainment aft. This complemented *QE2*'s activity programme and made the ship's somewhat difficult deck plan easier to navigate.

A number of Cunard signature rooms were created aboard *QE2* during Project Lifestyle. These included the Golden Lion Pub, Chartroom Bar and Bookshop, all of which are present on *Queen Mary 2*. 'Project Lifestyle' also introduced the Cunard Heritage Trail aboard *QE2*. Comprising Cunard memorabilia and

Left: In her new livery, *QE2* departs Southampton. (Michael Gallagher / Cunard)

Below: A view along the Quarter Deck Promenade, near the Library and Bookshop. (Frame / Cross)

artworks created to celebrate the line's past, the Heritage Trail created a sense of history and a strong connection between *QE2* and the liners of days gone by. Some of the more popular items included a large model of RMS *Mauretania*, which was placed outside the newly renamed Mauretania restaurant on Quarter Deck, the Boston (Britannia) Cup showcased outside the Yacht Club on Upper Deck, and the Laconia Cup, also located outside the Yacht Club.

Cunard intended to relaunch *QE2* again with post-refit bookings being marketed as 'The New *QE2*'. To symbolise this, the hull was repainted in Royal Blue (dark navy blue). A tricolour 'speed stripe' was added to the ship's superstructure between Quarter and One Deck. This and the Cunard Lion motif, a new addition on the forward hull, formed part of Cunard's revised identity and were also applied to other members of the fleet.

At the end of the thirty-two-day refit, *QE2* set sail for Southampton far from complete. Workers stayed aboard the ship in a vain attempt to finish the refit before her crossing to New York and subsequent Christmas cruise; however, there was far too much left to complete. Following her arrival in Southampton, HRH the Duke of York toured the new *QE2*. Noticing the unfinished state of the ship, he remarked, 'I think you are very brave to be going to sea this week.'

The British Maritime Safety Office inspected *QE2* while she was alongside in Southampton and issued a restricted

passenger certificate, limiting the vessel to carrying only 1,000 passengers. This led Cunard to inform over 460 booked passengers that they couldn't travel with *QE2*. The media picked up on the story and *QE2* started to make headlines around the world once again. Cunard attempted to remedy the situation by offering those affected a refund and future free cruise.

Those passengers who did sail aboard the ship had a less than perfect experience, with areas of *QE2* incomplete, problems with the ship's plumbing and an active workforce aboard; by the time the ship arrived in New York, word had spread regarding the incomplete condition of the vessel. The United States Coast Guard inspected *QE2* and issued a Certificate of Control Verification for a Foreign Vessel, and although the

issue leading to this action was quickly rectified, the resulting media storm painted *QE2* in a very poor light. In all, *QE2* ended 1994 with a tarnished name. However, once it was complete, Project Lifestyle's result was unarguably positive. The ship was reborn, and Cunard predicted that this work, along with her re-engining in 1986–87, would allow the ship to sail 'well into the twenty-first century'.

Above: The temporary Mauretania sign at the entry to the restaurant, following its name change from Caronia. (Frame / Cross)

Left: *QE2* and the Sydney Opera House during her 1995 call to the port. (Michael Gallagher / Cunard)

eleven

A NEW OWNER

She embodies the essence of British heritage
and all that is Cunard.

Larry Pimentel, Cunard president, on *QE2*
following her 1999 refit

January 1995 saw *QE2* embark on a world tour. Dubbed the Golden Route World Cruise, the voyage took her to the far corners of the globe and offered her legions of fans worldwide a chance to inspect the new interiors. With the refit work complete, the ship was looking vibrant and fresh and receiving high praise from critics and passengers alike.

However, 1995 was not all smooth sailing. On 11 September at 2.10 a.m. *QE2* was hit by a 90ft rogue wave generated by rough weather from nearby Hurricane Luis. Captain (later Commodore) Ronald Warwick was on the Bridge and directed *QE2*'s bow into the wave, considerably reducing the risk to the ship and those aboard. Commodore Warwick explains:

It looked as if we were heading straight for the White Cliffs of Dover. The wave seemed to take ages to reach us, but it was probably less than a minute before it broke with tremendous force over the bow of *QE2*. An incredible shudder went through the ship, followed a few moments later by two smaller shudders. At the same time, the sea was cascading all over the fore part of the ship, including the Bridge, and it was several seconds before it had drained away from the wheelhouse windows and the vision ahead was restored.

In 1996, *QE2* entered King George V dry dock in Southampton. Here, refurbishment work was completed which included finishing off the few remaining cabin bathrooms that had not been completed in 1994. That same year, Cunard's owner, Trafalgar House, was acquired by Kvaerner. The £904 million sale price included Trafalgar House's mixed portfolio, of which Cunard was a part. Kvaerner had no long-term interest in operating a cruise line and almost immediately the rumour mill activated, with regular stories suggesting Cunard and *QE2* might be sold off to other shipping lines.

Cunard's problems started to mount, with increasing competition from larger lines adding pressure to the company's bottom line. While cruise lines such as P&O, Princess and Royal Caribbean were specialising as well as investing in new ships, Cunard's fleet consisted of a mixed bag of ageing or second-hand vessels operating across a variety of markets. For example, *QE2* operated exclusively under the Cunard banner, offering transatlantic crossings and cruises aboard what was the last of the ocean liners at that time. *Sagafjord* and *Vistafjord* had been grouped with the *Royal Viking Sun* and ran under the Cunard–Royal Viking brand. Cunard's two super yachts, *Sea Goddess I* and *Sea Goddess II* were marketed under the Cunard–Sea Goddess brand, while the 4-star cruise ships *Cunard Countess*, *Cunard Princess*, *Cunard Crown Dynasty*

QE2 and *Caronia*, both freshly repainted in Cunard's traditional colours. (Michael Gallagher / Cunard)

and *Cunard Crown Jewel* were marketed as Cunard–Crown cruises. This situation was exacerbated when looking at the age and size of Cunard's tonnage. While *QE2* was a unique and well-differentiated ship, the other members of the fleet all competed in markets where a plethora of competitors often offered newer ships, cheaper prices or better cruises and itineraries. *Cunard Princess* was withdrawn from the fleet

in 1995, while in 1996 *Cunard Crown Jewel* ended her Cunard career. That same year *Sagafjord* was chartered to Transocean Tours. She was renamed *Gripsholm*, and when a fire broke out aboard the ship she was permanently withdrawn from Cunard's fleet and sold to Saga Cruises. By 1998 *Cunard Countess* and *Cunard Crown Dynasty* had also left the fleet. This left Cunard with five ships. The line attempted to market them as

The recreated Caronia restaurant as it was from 1999 to 2008. (Frame / Cross)

Above: *QE2* passes De syv søstrene (The Seven Sisters) in Norway. (Michael Gallagher / Cunard)

Right: *QE2* at anchor during another cruise. (Michael Gallagher / Cunard)

a combined luxury offering; the fleet consisting of five of the ten highest-rated cruise ships in the world. But the financial situation at Cunard was worsening, and rumours abounded that *QE2* would be sold to P&O or even retired and scrapped!

In April 1998 the cruise industry was greeted by the surprising yet welcome news that Carnival Corporation had acquired the controlling share of Cunard Line for US$500 million. Carnival

had identified the value of the Cunard brand as well as the goodwill that was generated by owning the world's best-loved ship. Carnival merged Cunard with fellow subsidiary Seabourn Cruises and set about reorganising the fleet. *Royal Viking Sun* and the *Sea Goddesses* were transferred to Seabourn's fleet, while *Vistafjord* was given a significant refurbishment, emerging as *Caronia*, resplendent in traditional Cunard livery.

QE2 was treated to a £30 million refurbishment, which included the complete recreation of the Caronia restaurant in a *Titanic*-esque style, leveraging the success of James Cameron's blockbuster movie. The refit was undertaken at the Lloyd Werft shipyard in Bremerhaven, Germany, and included the mammoth task of stripping back all of *QE2*'s hull paint. She was then repainted with a federal grey hull and white superstructure.

A HOME AT SEA

ISABELLE PRONDZYNSKI

MODERATOR AT The *QE2* STORY FORUM

Unlike many *QE2* fans, I fell in love with the ship slowly and over a period of many years.

My mother, a recent widow in 1998, had decided that cruising would allow her to combine her love of the sea with her need to take a rest, and to do so in the comfort of a ship with an excellent reputation. And so, one day, she set out in a tender to embark *QE2* at anchor off Dún Laoghaire. She enjoyed that cruise so much that next time she asked me to accompany her. And then my sister. And a family friend. And so a decade of annual *QE2* visits began.

At first, I enjoyed the leisurely family time on board, the comforts and the care we received, the sea and the ever-changing landscape around us as we visited ports and went on excursions. But as time went on, it was the ship herself that became the greatest attraction. The more I learnt about *QE2*, her history, her design and what made her special, the more I went on to discover for myself, relishing the days on board and following her by Bridgecam while away.

She had become a 'home' to us: a beloved and familiar place, where we knew the nooks and crannies, and kept discovering more, and where we knew many of the crew and were happy each time to see them again.

When she disappeared to Dubai, I was grateful to be asked to help moderate The *QE2* Story forum. Every day, this allows me to recall the ship as she was, learn more about her and help to keep her legend alive.

One of *QE2*'s classic tender boats is lowered from Boat Deck while the ship rests at anchor. (Michael Gallagher / Cunard)

QE2 at sea in her traditional livery. (Michael Gallagher / Cunard)

The ship all lit up at night. (Michael Gallagher / Cunard)

Furthermore, Carnival announced plans to build a new large transatlantic ocean liner, the first conceived since *QE2* entered service thirty years earlier. Cunard's president and chief operating officer Larry Pimentel was at pains to assure the public that the new ship, code-named Project Queen Mary, would not replace *QE2* in the foreseeable future. Project Queen Mary evolved into *Queen Mary 2*, a ship much larger than *QE2*. Her construction in France commenced in 2000 and lasted until 2003.

QE2 was given another multimillion-pound refit in 1999, emerging with a revitalised and refreshed internal appearance; with work designed to complement the Project Lifestyle refurbishment and ensure the ship had a secure future in the fast-paced modern world. Changes included the addition of new penthouse suites on Boat Deck and Two Deck, a reworked Purser's Office, updated sound, lighting and curtains in the Grand Lounge and updated colours in passenger cabins. The

Above: *QE2* in her role as a cruise ship visited the Caribbean most years as part of her Christmas / New Year schedule. (Michael Gallagher / Cunard)

Right: *QE2*'s cruising role took her to many more places than her predecessors. (Michael Gallagher / Cunard)

QE2 transited the Panama Canal thirty-nine times during her career. (Michael Gallagher / Cunard)

new suite on Boat Deck forward was built in a space previously occupied by the Radio Room. Named the Caledonia Suite, it was wheelchair accessible and employed modern aids to assist those in wheelchairs to access the cabin, bathrooms, curtains and television. The new suite created on Two Deck near the Midships Lobby was built in a space previously occupied by the hotel manager and cruise director's cabins. Once combined, it became the Aquitania Suite and its construction involved three large windows being cut into the hull.

The 1999 refit achieved the goal of further updating QE2 and preparing her for a new lease of life in the twenty-first century. Cunard's then president Larry Pimentel said of the works, 'As the flagship of Britain, QE2 will reflect the essence of Britain. The ship has a long life ahead of her and we are committed to maintaining, and improving further, the already high standards for which she is known.'

twelve

CRUISES, CROSSINGS AND CRASHES

This magnificent vessel, certainly the most famous ship in the world, will sail into the Millennium with new vigour.

Larry Pimentel, Cunard president

QE2 met the newly renamed *Caronia* off Barbados as part of the millennium celebrations. There, Cunard took the opportunity to photograph the two ships at close quarters; passengers lined the decks of both vessels to witness the historic rendezvous at sea.

On 4 July 2000, while manoeuvring in New York Harbor, *QE2* collided with the Japanese naval vessel *Kashima*. Berthing was made particularly difficult by the high number of boats in the harbour for Independence Day celebrations. After the event, a Japanese admiral commented that it was an 'honour to be kissed by a Queen'.

The following year in March, *QE2* called at Dubai during her maiden world voyage. While not her first call in the city, it was significant as her arrival was timed to coincide with the opening of the new Dubai Cruise Terminal.

Later in 2001, *QE2* undertook commemorative transatlantic crossings in honour of the 65th anniversary of RMS *Queen Mary*'s maiden voyage. The crossings included guests who had sailed aboard *Queen Mary* during her maiden voyage, with Cunard offering them the same fare as they had paid in 1936. Some tickets were as low as £70.20, as the original third-class price had been £70 4*s*.

The devastating terrorist attacks in the United States of America on 11 September 2001 sent shockwaves through the transportation industry, and cruise lines were not immune to the resulting downturn in international travel. *QE2* was a regular visitor to New York as part of her transatlantic crossings, and following the 9/11 attacks the ship used Boston as the American terminus of the transatlantic service. Boston was no stranger to Cunard liners. It had been the first port in the United States to accommodate Cunard's fleet, having been selected by Sir Samuel Cunard himself. *QE2* was the first major passenger ship to return to New York when she called there in early 2002.

On 20 November, *QE2* arrived in Bremerhaven for an overhaul. The $12 million refit included work to the ship's two most exclusive suites, as well as several restaurants and bars aboard.

During *QE2*'s 2002 world cruise the ship sailed in tandem with P&O's *Aurora* across the Great Australian Bight. During the passage, the weather conditions worsened. While the transatlantic-built *QE2* was able to maintain her cruising speed, the newer *Aurora* was slowed for the duration of the storm. At the end of her world cruise, on 26 April 2002 *QE2* called at Fort Lauderdale. Here, one of the original whistles from the RMS *Queen Mary* was loaded aboard the Cunard flagship for the voyage to Europe where it was later reconditioned and placed aboard the new *Queen Mary 2*.

Above and right: *QE2* and *Caronia* together off Barbados during the millennium celebrations. (Michael Gallagher / Cunard)

Above: Looking smart in her traditional livery, *QE2* is seen at sea. (Michael Gallagher / Cunard)

Left: *QE2* at sea in the year 2000. (Michael Gallagher / Cunard)

QE2 in Auckland as part of her 2003 world cruise. (Frame / Cross)

The following month, *QE2* was subject to a seawater leak that, had quick action not been taken, could have resulted in serious consequences for the ship. The leak was caused by seawater corrosion around the starboard seawater inlet pipe, which fed the evaporator used to create fresh water. The leak's location made a simple fix impossible, resulting in serious flooding. An ingenious solution was devised with an inflatable bag being inserted into the leaking pipe. Once inflated, it blocked the flow of water and stopped the flooding. *QE2* was then able to proceed safely to New York, where she arrived on 24 May. Here, she was permanently repaired.

In August 2002 *QE2* clocked 5 million nautical miles, at which time she became the most travelled passenger ship in history. The milestone coincided with a transatlantic crossing, and all passengers and crew aboard were given documentation of the event.

When the iconic and technologically unrivalled supersonic airliner Concorde retired from service in 2003, it brought an end to the Cunard–British Airways partnership. With

RETURNING TO *QE2*
COMMODORE WARWICK

I spent a substantial period of my career with Cunard appointed to *QE2*, serving on board at various times in all ranks from the position of second officer through to master. My period in command, although not continuous, spanned a record thirteen years, and as a result I have a strong affinity for the ship.

Although I had been happily retired for a couple of years, I was very pleased to be offered the job of taking over *QE2* on behalf of the new owners when the vessel arrived in Dubai. I accepted the position in October 2008 and at that time there was a possibility that the ship would go on from Dubai to Singapore in January 2009 to commence conversion work. The new Chief Engineer sailed with the ship from Southampton and several more deck and engineer officers joined in Alexandria for familiarisation.

After setting up all the safety and security procedures and familiarising the new crew, we set about cleaning the ship. To do this we employed four additional staff from Egypt. This team cleaned every single area on the ship from top to bottom. Because of baggage restrictions, many of the Cunard crew who had been serving on the ship for many years had left quite a few personal items in their cabins, including several thousand foreign coins. All these things were set aside and donated to the Dubai branch of the Mission to Seafarers. In the crew cabins and work areas we found numerous books and quite a few pieces of Cunard china, which were also donated to the Mission. By the time I left, the interior of the ship was in immaculate condition and anyone coming on board would have thought she was ready to sail on another voyage.

With a good multinational crew of only thirty-nine souls it was very peaceful, and I spent my spare time methodically visiting every part of the liner from the top of the funnel down to the end of the propeller tail shaft. I left *QE2* in January 2009 when it became clear that the plans to convert the ship had been abandoned for the time being.

QE2 performs high-speed manoeuvres during a dramatic early morning photoshoot in 2005. (Michael Gallagher / Cunard)

QE2's bow cuts through the ocean. (Michael Gallagher / Cunard)

a maiden flight that had coincided with the year of *QE2*'s maiden voyage, Concorde had never made good on its threat to annihilate all slower modes of transport. During Concorde's retirement flight on 24 October 2003, it passed over *QE2*'s position, prompting Captain Ray Heath to send the following message: 'From one British icon to another, *QE2* and Concorde have been an improbable, unique and successful transatlantic partnership for the past twenty years. We are sorry to see you go.'

All three right: *QE2* in Geirangerfjord in 2006. (Michael Gallagher / Cunard)

Above: At 963ft in length, *QE2* was often longer than the piers she encountered. (Michael Gallagher / Cunard)

Left: *QE2*'s Bridge photographed from the forepeak. Note the Cunard emblem on her superstructure. It was originally displayed aboard *Cunard Princess*. (Michael Gallagher / Cunard)

Right: *QE2* makes for a dramatic backdrop to this grassy field. (Michael Gallagher / Cunard)

Tour Guide

ENTERTAINMENT DECKS

Boat Deck

As the name suggests, Boat Deck was the location of *QE2*'s lifeboats. Twenty motorised boats were held on davits suspended above a teak-wood deck. On the deck, passengers could find wooden steamer deckchairs that were covered by Cunard-branded cushions each day by attentive deck staff.

Inside, Boat Deck housed a number of key public and private rooms. Forward, the Officers' Wardroom was one of the few places that offered a forward view over *QE2*'s bow. This room was reserved as a sanctuary for *QE2*'s senior crew. However, on special occasions selected passengers were invited to the 'Wardie' for cocktail functions.

Above: The Queens Grill restaurant in 2008. (Frame / Cross)

Left: The Project Lifestyle incarnation of *QE2*'s famous Queens Grill. (Michael Gallagher / Cunard)

Aft of the Wardroom and A Stairway, passengers would find the Queens Grill. Originally named The 736 Club, the room was recreated to become one of the finest restaurants at sea during the ship's 1972 refurbishment, accommodating diners from the newly added balcony suites. The Queens Grill restaurant was usually accessed from the separate Queens Grill Lounge. This lounge was an exclusive retreat for guests travelling in Q-grade accommodation, and was the way passengers could access the suite accommodation on Signal and Sun Decks. The lounge had large windows that overlooked the promenade deck and a bar

PORTRAIT OF PRINCESS ELIZABETH AND THE DUKE OF EDINBURGH
BOAT DECK

On the Boat Deck landing of D Stairway, port side, was a portrait of Princess Elizabeth and Prince Philip. It was originally displayed aboard RMS *Caronia*. Princess Elizabeth launched *Caronia* in 1949, the final public engagement she undertook before she married. (Frame / Cross)

PORTRAIT OF HM THE QUEEN MOTHER
BOAT DECK

Painted by Sir Oswald Birley, this portrait originally hung aboard RMS *Queen Elizabeth*. It was displayed aboard *QE2* from 1994 until 2008 and remained with the ship when she arrived in Dubai. (Frame / Cross)

that served drinks and canapés throughout the day and night.

For those wishing to access movies or daytime theatre shows, the Theatre Balcony on Boat Deck offered a raised view into the main theatre on Upper Deck, while the ship's Boardroom was located on the port side of the Theatre Balcony.

QE2's shopping hub was found on Boat Deck, with the Royal Promenade surrounding the Grand Lounge void. Brand names such as Christian Dior, Cartier, Bally and Harrods could be found here, while in the evenings passengers would sit on red fabric chairs to watch the show on the Grand Lounge stage, one deck down.

Above: Lifeboats 1 and 2 were painted red and were rapid-deployment craft, located close to the Bridge to enable easy access for the officers. (Frame / Cross)

Above: The lifeboats, stored above Boat Deck, offered shelter and shade for those below. (Frame / Cross)

Left: The sports centre included traditional shipboard games such as shuffleboard. (Frame / Cross)

HERITAGE
TRAIL

THE TAPESTRIES
BOAT DECK

Three unique tapestries were created by Swedish tapestry artist Helena Hernmarck in honour of *QE2*'s launch. The trio comprised an image of HM Queen Elizabeth II, *QE2*'s bow during the launch and the ship in the River Clyde. Following the Project Lifestyle refurbishment, the tapestries were displayed on the Boat Deck landing of E Stairway. However, many regular *QE2* travellers remember their previous location on display outside the Columbia restaurant. (Frame / Cross)

Upper Deck

Much of *QE2*'s passenger activity was concentrated on Upper Deck and Quarter Deck, with Upper Deck housing a number of favourites. When *QE2* entered service in 1969, Upper Deck primarily housed public rooms for tourist-class passengers.

The aft end of Upper Deck was the evening entertainment hub, housing the Yacht Club Bar. Originally named the Double Down Bar, the room was completely rebuilt in 1986–87 and renamed the Yacht Club. The updated space featured a bar around a custom-built glass Steinway baby grand piano. Enlarged and redecorated again in 1994, the room was transformed into a peaceful daytime sanctuary that became a nightclub after dark. The updated Yacht Club featured a bar on the port side, which sported twin sail features resembling the hull of a yacht. Raised seating areas on both the port and starboard sides of the room overlooked a central seating area and dance floor where the ship's DJ and Caribbean band would play into the small hours. In the Yacht Club the music didn't end until the last passenger had left the dance floor!

Forward of the Yacht Club were a number of *QE2*'s Heritage Trail items, including

The Grand Lounge was first created in 1987, as seen here. It replaced the Double Down Room. (Michael Gallagher / Cunard)

the Boston (Britannia) Cup (1994–2004) and a model of RMS *Britannia*. During the ship's 1994 refurbishment, *QE2* had been transformed into a museum-at-sea, with hundreds of artefacts representing Cunard's illustrious history placed aboard, and these items formed just a small part of the trail. This area led into the G Stairway lobby.

Lovers of table tennis could have a game, with tables located on the port-side aft indoor promenade of Upper Deck. On the starboard side, the Tour and Travel Office was the place to visit to book shore tours or arrange transfers for your post-cruise travels.

Both promenades led into the Grand Lounge. Originally called the Double Down Room, this space was completely rebuilt twice during the ship's career. Its first use was as the tourist-class lounge, where after-dinner dancing and cabaret shows could be enjoyed. The space was finished in a 1960s style, with chrome, leather and glass used extensively throughout. Following the ship's 1986–87 refurbishment it emerged with terraced seating, a central bandstand surrounded by twin staircases and a star-lit ceiling that twinkled at night. It was again rebuilt in 1994, when, along with most of *QE2*'s other interior spaces, it was redecorated in a more sedate style. This saw the stage expanded as well as an extensive sound and lighting update. The twin staircases were removed and an extension was added to G Stairway, allowing passengers to access the Boat Deck level.

QE2's casino (shown here in its 1987–94 fit-out) was a popular venue for those wishing to test their luck. (Michael Gallagher / Cunard)

HERITAGE TRAIL

PETER RADMORE'S CUNARD COLLECTION
UPPER DECK

Located just off the D Stairway landing of Upper Deck, near the Casino, was the Peter Radmore Collection. Comprising just a small part of his Cunard memorabilia, the display included Tri-ang models, plates, menus, ashtrays, pens, cutlery and other rare items from Cunard's history. The collection was bequeathed to Cunard when Mr Radmore died. (Frame / Cross)

HERITAGE
TRAIL

MODEL OF *BRITANNIA*
UPPER DECK

The first ship designed and built for the four-ship regular transatlantic service, *Britannia* is often noted as being Cunard's first vessel. She was a twin-paddle steam-powered liner with a top speed of 9 knots. *Britannia* and her fleet mates could complete the transatlantic voyage in fourteen days. Powered by a steam engine that drove two large paddle wheels, she was a single-funnelled liner. A model of *Britannia* was displayed in a custom glass cabinet outside the Yacht Club on Upper Deck. (Frame / Cross)

The Crystal Bar was added in 1994 and became an instant success. (Frame / Cross)

Forward of the Grand Lounge on the port side was *QE2*'s casino. Originally named the Players Club, the casino included slot machines and tables with croupiers. During the day, activities included 'how to' classes for some of the classic games, while at night, this area became a popular after-dinner location for people wanting to test their luck.

On the starboard side was the Golden Lion Pub. Built in 1994, it was a controversial addition to *QE2* that replaced the popular Theatre Bar. Designed to resemble a traditional English pub, many *QE2* regulars felt it was out of place aboard the last of the great transatlantic liners. However, the Golden Lion became an extremely popular venue, with live entertainment, a lunchtime meal service and beer on tap. Towards the end of *QE2*'s career, large TV screens were installed in the pub to broadcast live sport for fans to enjoy.

Forward of the Golden Lion was the Theatre. This space changed little during *QE2*'s career, and featured a large movie screen, a stage and a podium. Here, *QE2*'s extensive and well-respected enrichment programme was

The Britannia Grill was one of the highest-rated restaurants aboard *QE2*. (Frame / Cross)

QUEEN MARY TRIBUTE
UPPER DECK

On the Upper Deck landing of
G Stairway was a large cabinet that held
a tribute to the original RMS *Queen
Mary*. Key features included an original
Queen Mary lifebuoy, a large model
of the ship, menus, playing cards and
napkins. (Frame / Cross)

hosted, and saw guest speakers covering topics from ocean liner history to the origins of the universe. Movies were shown in the Theatre, as well as the occasional broadcast of special events, including the wedding of HRH Prince Charles and Lady Diana Spencer in 1981. Seating was arranged over two levels, Upper Deck and Boat Deck, and included classic fold-down cinema seats. The Theatre was also home to a full-size grand piano, which sat permanently on the stage. In fact, the piano was so large it couldn't be removed from the Theatre without being dismantled.

The Crystal Bar, created in 1994, was the forward-most bar on Upper Deck and spanned the full width of the ship. Modelled after the Observation Lounge aboard RMS *Queen Elizabeth*, the bar was a peaceful retreat during the day, and a busy pre-dinner hub in the evening. The Crystal Bar was designed to service three of the ship's restaurants, Princess Grill, Britannia Grill and Mauretania restaurant. While the two grills were located below the bar, on Quarter Deck, they were accessed through twin staircases from the Crystal Bar. Similarly, the Crystal Bar led into

THE BOSTON (BRITANNIA) CUP
UPPER DECK

The 2½ft-tall Boston Cup (also known as the Britannia Cup) was on display outside the Yacht Club from 1994 until 2004. The silver cup was designed by master craftsmen in Boston and intended as a gift for Sir Samuel Cunard. It was to be presented to him aboard RMS *Britannia* after she made her maiden call to Boston in 1840.

However, the cup was not completed in time for *Britannia*'s arrival. The whereabouts of the cup is sketchy from this period until 1967, when a Cunard director stumbled upon it in a Maryland antique shop. Recognising its significance in the Cunard story, he acquired the cup and had it installed aboard *Franconia* until *QE2* entered service. It was then transferred across to *QE2* where it was displayed in the Columbia restaurant for many years. Following the 1994 refurbishment, the Boston Cup was relocated to the aft end of Upper Deck, just outside the Yacht Club. Here, it was displayed in a specially designed and lit cabinet as part of the Cunard Heritage Trail. It remained with *QE2* until 2004, when it was symbolically handed over to be displayed aboard the newly crowned flagship. It remains aboard *QM2* to this day. (Frame / Cross)

The Columbia restaurant following the 1987 refit. Aside from some colour changes, it was largely the same as the 1969 design. (Michael Gallagher / Cunard)

the Mauretania restaurant, which occupied the forward end of Upper Deck.

The Mauretania restaurant was the most renamed room aboard *QE2*, starting life as the Britannia restaurant, serving tourist-class passengers, it was rebuilt as Tables of the World restaurant in 1977 and again as Mauretania restaurant in 1987. During the 1994 refit, the restaurant was recreated as the Caronia restaurant, and allocated to passengers holding a C-grade cabin. Similarly, Mauretania guests were relocated to the former Columbia restaurant on Quarter Deck. This was considered a better location for single-seating diners, while allowing Caronia passengers to share the Crystal Bar with the Princess and Britannia Grill diners. The restaurant was completely rebuilt, with large glass room divides, a mural of RMS *Caronia* at a tropical location and a large model of *Caronia* at the entry. The centrepiece of the room was a large sculpture depicting the

'white horses of the Atlantic' – an artistic take on the shape formed as waves break on the bow of a ship underway. Despite the room being completely rebuilt, large numbers of regular C-grade passengers were not happy with the change of dining venue, and by April 1997 the restaurant was once again swapped, regaining its name of Mauretania. Initially, a large model of RMS *Caronia* remained the centrepiece of the newly renamed restaurant, causing some confusion for passengers exploring *QE2*'s Heritage Trail. Following the 1999 refit, a *Mauretania* model took pride of place in the restaurant, while a mural on the forward bulkhead was repainted to remove references to *Caronia*.

Forward of the Mauretania restaurant was A Stairway. This stairway led up to Boat Deck, and all the way down to Five Deck. There were no landings at Quarter Deck or One Deck, as it passed through the galley and crew areas on those two decks.

Quarter Deck

When *QE2* was built, Quarter Deck primarily housed public rooms designated for first-class passengers. Like Upper Deck, it was dedicated to passenger public rooms, with no passenger cabins housed on this deck.

At the forward end of Quarter Deck, the first passenger spaces were the Princess Grill (port) and Britannia Grill (starboard). The Princess Grill was part of *QE2*'s 1969 design. Originally named The Grill Room, the Princess Grill was the original first-class restaurant aboard and held this status until the Queens Grill was built on Boat Deck in 1972. Inside this room were four statues by Janine Janet depicting 'The Four Elements' – fire, earth, air and water. It is rumoured that Janet created a fifth element, Venus; however, it was never installed aboard *QE2*.

The Princess Grill was one of the few places aboard that still resembled the original 1969 vision for the ship by the time *QE2* retired. The split-level restaurant endured a stint as an overflow dining space for the Columbia restaurant following the introduction of the Queens Grill, before being restored as an independent restaurant in 1976. It then remained in operation until *QE2* retired.

The decor was dominated by red hues and combined specially designed *QE2* race chairs with wooden-clad booth seating along the centre wall. Following the 1999 refit, newly designed wooden chairs that resembled the style used aboard older Cunard ships such as *Aquitania* and *Mauretania* supplemented the original furnishings. The restaurant was originally accessed from the intimate Princess

The Caronia restaurant bears no resemblance to the original Columbia restaurant that once occupied this space. (Frame / Cross)

HERITAGE
TRAIL

QUEEN MARY PIANO
QUARTER DECK

An original piano from RMS *Queen Mary* resided in *QE2*'s Chartroom Bar from 1994 through to 2008. It was tuned regularly and played each evening. (Pam Massey)

Grill Lounge on One Deck. Passengers could enjoy pre-dinner champagne in the lounge before ascending to the Grill Room one deck above via a spiral staircase. There was also a lift included for disabled passenger use.

Immediately opposite the Princess Grill on the starboard side of the ship was the Britannia Grill. Added to *QE2* in 1990, the restaurant was originally named Princess Grill II but was quickly renamed Princess Grill Starboard to remove the false belief that it was a lower grade of restaurant than Princess Grill Port. In 1994 it was renamed Britannia Grill, in honour of Cunard's first ship. Finished in blues, Britannia Grill was very different in style and design to its Princess Grill counterpart. However, similarly to Princess Grill, the restaurant was accessible via a chrome L-shaped staircase that linked it to Upper Deck's Crystal Bar. A scale model

of RMS *Britannia* featured in Britannia Grill's entry, while full-length windows offered uninterrupted views of the ocean.

In fact, one of the unique design features of *QE2* was the abundance of natural light in all of her dining spaces. This was achieved through the use of aluminium in the construction of *QE2*'s superstructure, lightening the ship and thus allowing the heavier restaurants and public rooms to be placed on higher decks than on the original Cunard Queens.

Aft of the Princess and Britannia Grills was the Caronia restaurant. Named Columbia when *QE2* was first placed into service, the restaurant remained the domain of first-class passengers until 1994, when it was refurbished to become Mauretania. For the next three years, the restaurant served those holding an M-class ticket, until Cunard opted

The Chartroom Bar replaced the Midships Bar in 1994 and featured a backlit map of the North Atlantic Ocean. (Frame / Cross)

to restore the venue as a C-class restaurant after a backlash from regular guests.

As Columbia, the restaurant played host to a variety of special events, including visits by HM the Queen Mother in 1988, and by HM the Queen and HRH the Duke of Edinburgh in 1990.

Fans of British television's *Keeping up Appearances* will remember the Columbia as the restaurant that hosted the captain's table in the episode 'Sea Fever' – this was indeed a feature of Columbia. The Boston Cup was also displayed in this restaurant until 1994.

During its brief stint as Mauretania, the restaurant played host to a model of RMS *Mauretania*, while outside the venue, on the D Stairway landing, a giant model of the same ship was on display.

When the restaurant reverted to C-class clientele, it was renamed Caronia, taking its name from Cunard's famous 'Green Goddess', which entered service in 1949. The space was originally redecorated in a green art deco theme, with a backlit false ceiling that gave the space a dramatic appearance. It was finally completely redesigned in 1999 to create a more intimate, traditional-looking ocean-liner space, with chandeliers, wooden chairs and rich furnishings as well as a detailed mural on the forward wall. The Caronia restaurant was accessible from the D Stairway landing.

On the port side of Quarter Deck, *QE2*'s immensely popular library and bookshop could be found. Originally a library and card room, this area was rebuilt during the 1994 refit to create a warm, welcoming space. The bookshop was situated just forward of the library, and was the first of its kind at sea. Developed specially for *QE2* by boutique book retailer Ocean Books, it stocked an enviable range of maritime books, maritime

art and *QE2*-branded trinkets, as well as novels and other non-fiction titles. The library itself was the largest at sea until *QM2* entered service, with over 6,000 books. Its design and decor mirrored the bookshop, although the room was dominated by a cut-away model of *Aquitania*, which formed part of the Cunard Heritage Trail. Among the delights of the bookshop and library were the large windows that overlooked the Quarter Deck promenade. Here, books were displayed, and when an author was travelling aboard *QE2* a gold 'Author on Board' sign was proudly shown along with the author's books.

In the equivalent position on the starboard side of Quarter Deck, the Chartroom Bar offered a relaxing location to meet friends for a drink. One of the few bars aboard *QE2* to allow smoking, it was popular with Caronia diners due to its close proximity to the restaurant entry. This area was originally called the Midships Bar, but was recreated during the 1994 refit. Alterations included the addition of a backlit glass map of the North Atlantic Ocean, showing the various routes that *QE2* took between New York and Southampton, new glass panels and a refreshed interior decor.

Aft of the Chartroom Bar and spanning the width of the ship was the Queens Room. Originally conceived as the First-class Ballroom, the Queens Room sported a bold design including a honeycomb ceiling backlit in multiple colours and supported by large white 'trumpet' pillars. This, combined with specially designed futuristic-looking chairs and tables, made this space a distinct departure from the main ballrooms of *QE2*'s predecessors. However, as time went on, the room was altered, resulting in a mismatch

BUST OF HM THE QUEEN
QUARTER DECK

Crafted by Oscar Newman, the bust of HM Queen Elizabeth II was originally finished in bronze, but following Project Lifestyle in 1994, it emerged in a gold finish. It resided in the Queens Room for the duration of *QE2*'s career. Today it can be found aboard MV *Queen Elizabeth*. (Frame / Cross)

of designs and styles. As such, in the 1994 and 1999 refits the space was recreated, and sported a subtler decor by the time *QE2* retired – though the original ceiling and 'trumpet' columns remained.

Tucked into an alcove behind the Queens Room was Club 2000. Added in the 1994 refit, this space was dedicated to arcade games for kids and teens to enjoy. Parties were held here, with foosball and air hockey tables added in later years. By the time *QE2* retired, Club 2000 had been closed down and repurposed as a storeroom.

The final passenger area on Quarter Deck was the Lido restaurant. Originally called Club Lido, the space once included a swimming pool, which from 1983 sported a retractable glass roof known as a magrodome. While the roof allowed for the pool to be used in all weather conditions, it created a greenhouse effect in the Lido and as such was removed in 1994. At this time, the entire space was refurbished to resemble a winter garden, with wooden floors and wicker furniture. This proved impractical due to the motion of the ship and the floors were subsequently carpeted.

Six Deck and Seven Deck

QE2's Gymnasium was found on Seven Deck.
(Anders Johannessen)

While mainly dedicated to crew use, Six Deck housed two key passenger areas: the ship's hospital and the QE2 Spa. The hospital was accessible off C Stairway. Its location on Six Deck led to the phrase 'C-Six' being used to direct people to the hospital – a play on 'seasick'. Further aft and accessible from F Stairway, the QE2 Spa facility combined a thalassotherapy pool with treatment rooms, saunas and shower facilities. This space was originally one of *QE2*'s two indoor pools, but was greatly rebuilt during the post-Falklands refit, emerging then as the Golden Door Spa at Sea. Steiner's of London later took over the running of the spa, which was a popular place for both new and repeat guests.

The lowest deck that passengers could access, Seven Deck was again largely the domain of the crew. When *QE2* first came into service she had two indoor swimming

pools, one for first class and the other for tourist class. While the tourist-class pool on Six Deck was rebuilt into the QE2 Spa, the first-class pool on Seven Deck was retained throughout *QE2*'s career. Accessible from the C Stairway, it included a swimming pool, aerobics room and gymnasium. The saltwater pool was popular throughout *QE2*'s career,

being both heated and sheltered, allowing for constant use regardless of the weather. The ship's gym included a range of Cybex weight- and strength-building equipment, and Life Fitness cardio machines such as treadmills, steppers and cross trainers, and a Concept 2 rowing machine. There were towels available for use as well as chilled water.

QE2's indoor swimming pool on Seven Deck. (Anders Johannessen)

thirteen

FLAGSHIP NO MORE

From April 2004, *QE2* will be deployed
permanently on Southampton-based cruises.
She is still, and will continue to be, the fastest
passenger liner in service.

Pamela Conover, Cunard president

Cunard officially accepted *Queen Mary 2* into its fleet on 22 December 2003. The longest, tallest, widest and most expensive passenger ship built at the time was also the first true transatlantic liner created since *QE2* had entered service over thirty years earlier.

QM2 entered Southampton for the first time on 26 December 2003 and, following a gala naming ceremony on 12 January 2004, entered active service. However, unlike the three Cunard Queens before her, *QM2*'s maiden transatlantic crossing was not a direct express service from Southampton to New York. Rather, she took a leisurely crossing to Fort Lauderdale before commencing a series of cruises from ports in the United States. This gave *QE2* a reprieve, with the older Cunarder retaining her status as flagship until *QM2* returned to Southampton in April. To this end, on 25 April 2004 *QE2* met *QM2* in New York Harbor for what was the first of many royal rendezvous. This occasion was the first time in over forty years that two Cunard *Queens* had been berthed together in New York. That evening, the two Cunard *Queens* departed New York and commenced a tandem transatlantic crossing. Throughout the voyage the two vessels were within close visual range of each other, swapping positions so that all passengers aboard both ships were offered excellent views throughout the crossing.

Upon their arrival in Southampton, a ceremony was held aboard *QE2*. After a speech by then deputy Prime Minister John Prescott, Captain Ian McNaught of *QE2* handed the Boston (Britannia) Cup to Commodore Ronald Warwick of *QM2*, symbolically signifying that the newer liner had become flagship of the Cunard fleet.

The newly demoted *QE2* sailed that afternoon for Bremerhaven. Here, she was refurbished over twenty-one days with the aim of updating the vessel for her new role as a full-time cruise ship. Special attention was paid to areas of *QE2* that could be upgraded to suit the cruising role. This included the installation of new air-conditioning units, which included a large air intake on the roof of Signal Deck, somewhat changing *QE2*'s external appearance. Further work was conducted on Sun Deck aft, where a greatly underutilised sheltered deck was transformed into an outdoor bar. Named Funnel Bar (due to its location in the shadow of the ship's iconic funnel), the new venue was an instant hit on summer cruises and featured draught beer taps, live music and comfortable seating.

On 5 November 2004, *QE2* became the longest-serving transatlantic express liner in Cunard's history. The record had previously been held by *Aquitania*, which had a career as notable as *QE2*'s, having served in two world wars and survived

Right: Commodore Ronald Warwick and Captain Ian McNaught shake hands as *QE2* relinquishes her flagship status to *QM2*. (Michael Gallagher / Cunard)

Below: *QM2* and *QE2* in Southampton. (Michael Gallagher / Cunard)

Left: *QE2* alongside at the Queen Elizabeth II terminal. (Michael Gallagher / Cunard)

Above: *QE2*'s five-bladed variable-pitch propellers seen in her 2004 refit. (Kenny Campbell)

Below left: The ship's two bow thrusters. Note that the bow thruster doors are removed in this image. (Kenny Campbell)

Below: A worker strips paint from *QE2*'s Two Deck level. (Kenny Campbell)

Work is well under way to clear *QE2*'s hull of fifty-seven layers of paint! (Kenny Campbell)

The bare steel (darker colour) and aluminium alloy (lighter colour) are visible in this image from 2004. (Kenny Campbell)

QE2's bulbous bow in the dry dock, 2004. (Kenny Campbell)

A rare view of the ship's bottom. (Kenny Campbell)

QE2, looking rather awkward with her paint stripped, sits in the dry dock in 2004. (Kenny Campbell)

the Great Depression to become a household name. *QE2* also surpassed *Scythia*'s service record in 2005. *Scythia* was an intermediate liner operating on the secondary Atlantic services between New York and the Mediterranean, as well as London to Quebec, and previously held the record as the longest-serving Cunard Atlantic liner. While five other vessels in Cunard's history had served longer careers than *QE2*, they were not Atlantic liners, thus *QE2*'s long-service record meant she was not only the longest-serving Cunard express liner, but also the Cunard transatlantic liner with the most years in service.

Although *QE2* had been replaced by *QM2* on the transatlantic service, she still conducted occasional transatlantic crossings, with an annual crossing to New York in winter to prepare for her world cruise. These winter crossings attracted a unique bunch of thrill-seekers known as the 'Winter Crossing Club'. Their passion for the ship and her ability to handle high seas drew them to book these crossings, when the chances of heavy weather were far higher than during a summer voyage.

During the 2005 world cruise, while *QE2* was alongside in Fremantle, a group of rowdy locals snuck on to the pier and

Left, top and bottom: *QE2* alongside in Sydney, 2005. (Frame / Cross)

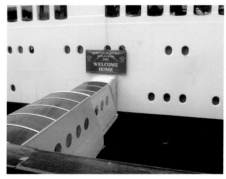

Above: *QE2* always carried a 'welcome home' sign to greet guests returning from shore tours. (Frame / Cross)

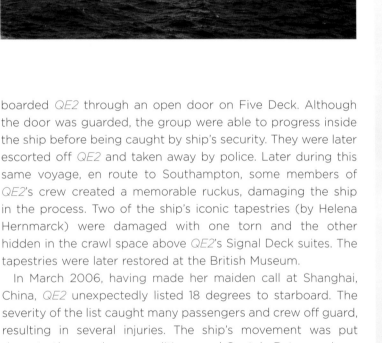

Left: *QE2* making her departure from Fremantle, 2005. (Frame / Cross)

Below: During overnight calls on her world cruise, such as those at Sydney and Hong Kong, workers would wire up the funnel to allow it to be painted. (Frame / Cross)

boarded *QE2* through an open door on Five Deck. Although the door was guarded, the group were able to progress inside the ship before being caught by ship's security. They were later escorted off *QE2* and taken away by police. Later during this same voyage, en route to Southampton, some members of *QE2*'s crew created a memorable ruckus, damaging the ship in the process. Two of the ship's iconic tapestries (by Helena Hernmarck) were damaged with one torn and the other hidden in the crawl space above *QE2*'s Signal Deck suites. The tapestries were later restored at the British Museum.

In March 2006, having made her maiden call at Shanghai, China, *QE2* unexpectedly listed 18 degrees to starboard. The severity of the list caught many passengers and crew off guard, resulting in several injuries. The ship's movement was put down to the rough sea conditions, and Captain Bates made an address over the ship's loud speakers to reassure passengers.

Later that year, *QE2* undertook what would be her final refurbishment at Lloyd Werft, Bremerhaven. This time, the yard was employed to update and refresh carpeting, and upholstery and also to repair the aluminium superstructure.

THE SLEEPING BEAUTY

ROB LIGHTBODY

FOUNDER OF THE *QE2* STORY FORUM

In April 2011, I was temporarily in between jobs with a bit of spare time on my hands. I had developed a relationship with the team managing *QE2* in Dubai over the previous two and a half years, as we together brought some accuracy to the online rumours about the ship's condition on The *QE2* Story forum. I asked to go aboard to document the ship's condition and was astounded when they said yes. I'm not normally a spontaneous person, but within days I was being picked up at Dubai airport and being whisked towards *QE2*. They were proud of the work they were doing on her, and wanted word to get out. I will never forget what followed over the next three days, and it is hard to summarise briefly.

Pulling up alongside the ship, she looked utterly unchanged. V-Ships were taking amazing care of her exterior. Stepping aboard again also felt just the same, although that was to change. She was so empty of human life and was 'undressed', artwork removed ... the sparkle had gone inside. However, I've always been most interested in *QE2* as a machine – a piece of engineering – and in that respect she was just the same.

Cunard, however, had left her. She had a new crew who considered her home after more than two years of caring for her and who were immensely proud of her. They quickly became my friends. It wasn't just a job for them, like it hadn't just been a job for their Cunard predecessors. I had access to all areas for three days. It wasn't enough time: I could have filled a week. As I left the ship, I was hugely optimistic for her. She was fine. She was waiting. I called the DVD of photos from the ship *Sleeping Beauty*, because that's how she seemed to me.

My frustration was because I had been on board the SS *Rotterdam* Cruise Hotel and it was easy to see how *QE2* could become the same, but Dubai didn't feel like the right place for an old British transatlantic liner. Visitors to Dubai want new shiny things. The only time I thought she might work there was when I was sitting on the boat deck in the cooler evenings, looking over the twinkling Dubai skyline and wishing there was a cold beer on board.

fourteen

SAYING GOODBYE

After such an illustrious career, we feel that the
time will be right for her to leave the fleet ...
However, she will not disappear.

Excerpt from the letter sent by Carol Marlow, Cunard's then
president and managing director, to *QE2*'s passengers
when the ship's retirement was announced

The 40th anniversary of *QE2*'s launch took place on 20 September 2007. This event was a key date in *QE2*'s 2007 itinerary, with a special voyage arranged to sail around Great Britain in celebration of the ship and her achievements over what was a truly remarkable career.

QE2's year started on a high note, with a series of special events planned as part of her world cruise. When *QE2* entered Sydney Harbour on 20 February 2007 the harbour city was already abuzz with excitement. Earlier that day, *QM2* had made her maiden arrival in the port and as the largest passenger ship to ever visit Australia she attracted a large crowd. *QE2*'s arrival was set for later in the day, with the two ships due to pass each other before sunset. The event had been well marketed, so a crowd was expected. However, no one could have anticipated the number of people that descended on Sydney to witness the first meeting of two Cunard Queens since RMS *Queen Mary* and RMS *Queen Elizabeth* met in the harbour during the Second World War. Crowds grew throughout the day so that by the time *QE2* arrived, over 1 million people were estimated to have lined the banks of the harbour, or taken to small pleasure craft. The festivities culminated in a spectacular fireworks display, after which the giant *QM2* departed the harbour, leaving *QE2* to overnight at the Overseas Passenger Terminal at Circular Quay.

When *QE2* returned to Southampton at the end of her world cruise, she settled into her usual season of European-based cruising. The ship was always a firm favourite of Southampton, and locals as well as 'ship-spotters' from far-flung corners of the globe would marvel at the sight of the graceful Cunard Queen departing or arriving in the busy cruise port.

On 10 June 2007 the ship set sail on her annual Voyage of the Vikings cruise. The trip departed from Southampton and called at Reykjavik, Isafjordur, Akureiri and Trondheim before arriving at Alesund, Norway, on 18 June. That day is one that will be long remembered by those passengers aboard, as each received a letter from Cunard's then president and managing director Carol Marlow. The letter explained that *QE2* had been sold to Istithmar, the investment arm of Dubai World, with the date of her final Southampton departure set for 11 November 2008. In the letter, Marlow commented: 'We think it is very important that *QE2* should end her seagoing career with dignity. We are, therefore, very pleased to have secured a permanent home for her that will enable future generations to continue to experience fully both the ship and her history.'

Captain Ian McNaught was in command of *QE2* for that voyage. As her master, the role had fallen on him to brief his officers and crew the night before. Emotions were high aboard

QE2 passes *QM2* in Sydney, 2007. (Michael Gallagher / Cunard)

QM2, *Queen Victoria* and *QE2* depart New York in tandem, 2008. (Michael Gallagher / Cunard)

QE2 and *Queen Victoria* pass one another in Sydney, 2008. (Michael Gallagher / Cunard)

the ship for the remainder of the voyage as both passengers and crew grappled with the revelation.

News spread fast around the world, as press releases were translated into an array of news items. At the centre of the story was information about the dramatic transformation that awaited *QE2* in Dubai. This included news that the ship may be returned to her original 1960s interior design. Ashore, as well as aboard *QE2*, frenzy erupted to secure a berth for the final voyages. Cunard had arranged several special voyages to take place in 2008, including a farewell tandem return crossing with *QM2* and an honorary lap around Great Britain.

Some passengers who had booked first-time cruises on *QE2* for 2008 now found they had secured a place in history, while her final voyage to Dubai sold out in thirty-six minutes. But despite the sadness of the ship's retirement, there was over a year left on *QE2*'s seagoing schedule including a 'round Britain' cruise in honour of the 40th anniversary of the ship's launch. The voyage called at a number of British ports, including Greenock, near where the liner was built. The 2008 voyage, originally marketed as the 'South America, Pacific and Orient Odyssey', was quickly

renamed '*QE2*'s Final World Cruise', despite it not being a full circumnavigation of the globe. Following the retirement announcement, the remaining cabins quickly sold out.

This voyage commenced with a tandem westbound transatlantic crossing in partnership with the new *Queen Victoria*. A meeting of three Cunard Queens in New York Harbor followed their arrival, when the two smaller Cunarders were joined by the *QM2*. *QE2* then proceeded westbound with farewell celebrations in almost every port she visited, the southern hemisphere celebrations for the ship being particularly special. When *QE2* called in Sydney she rendezvoused with *Queen Victoria* in a repeat of the very successful 'Meeting of the Queens' from 2007. The ship completed a farewell lap of Australia with huge crowds turning out in Melbourne, Hobart, Adelaide and Fremantle.

Interestingly, despite the ship's long service career, she still managed to make several maiden arrivals in her final months. One such occasion occurred in Albany, Australia, on 4 March 2008. During this call, thousands of people gathered on Mount Clarence to view the ship, while an honorary cannon was fired to welcome her to the port.

QE2 pulls away from Woolloomooloo while *Queen Victoria* manoeuvres near the Opera House, Sydney. (Michael Gallagher / Cunard)

QE2 and *Queen Victoria* pass by each other near Fort Dennison. (Michael Gallagher / Cunard)

QE2 made her maiden call at Albany on her final visit to Australia.
(Frame / Cross)

QE2 berthed in Southampton for the final time on the morning of 11 November 2008. (Andy Fitzsimmons)

QE2's last day in Southampton was on 11 November 2008. One million poppies were dropped over the vessel in honour of Remembrance Day. (Andy Fitzsimmons)

A fireworks display ended what was an emotional farewell from Southampton to *QE2*. (Andy Fitzsimmons)

Having departed Australian waters forever, *QE2* crossed the equator for the last time on her way to Singapore. From here, she headed north before transiting the Pacific Ocean. She arrived in Los Angeles on 30 March to bid a final farewell to the west coast of the United States. After a call at Acapulco, Mexico, *QE2* bid farewell to the Pacific Ocean for the final time, transiting the Panama Canal eastbound on 5 April and arriving back in Southampton on 18 April.

QE2 had originally been scheduled to undertake a fifteen-day refurbishment at Bremerhaven, Germany. However, with her withdrawal from service just months away, this refit was cancelled. Rather, a shorter refurbishment was undertaken alongside in Southampton. Work included re-carpeting and cleaning many areas of the ship, re-covering of seating in various lounges and restaurants, paintwork and a change to the colour of the seating in the Midships Lobby and Chartroom Bar. During this refit, *Queen Victoria* and *QM2* met *QE2* for the final three-Queen rendezvous. During this call, *QM2* passed by *QE2* and *Queen Victoria*, with all three ships sounding their whistles time and time again.

An Emirates A380-800 makes a low pass over *QE2* as she arrives in her new home of Dubai. (Michael Gallagher / Cunard)

On 2 June, HM Queen Elizabeth II visited *QE2* for the final time.

The ship completed a farewell lap of Great Britain as well as her final transatlantic crossings. These were completed in tandem with *QM2*, and at the completion of the voyages *QE2* had bid farewell to the United States of America for the last time.

When *QE2* entered Southampton for the final time on 11 November 2008, she ran aground on a sandbank. This was seen by many as 'the ship refusing to leave Southampton'. She was quickly refloated and made her way alongside to the Queen Elizabeth II Terminal. Divers inspected the underside of the hull and deemed the ship safe to sail. Her final day in Southampton was subject to several special events, including a farewell visit from HRH the Duke of Edinburgh. Following a comprehensive tour of the liner, Prince Philip was escorted on to *QE2*'s aft decks to witness 1 million poppies being dropped in honour of Remembrance Day.

A final fireworks display as *QE2*'s passengers and crew enjoy their last night aboard the ship. (Michael Gallagher / Cunard)

QE2 departed Southampton that evening amid much fanfare. A fireworks display was overshadowed by the beauty and elegance of the fully illuminated *QE2* pulling away from her berth and heading out to sea.

Her final voyage took her to Lisbon, Gibraltar, Civitavecchia, Naples, Valletta, Alexandria and the Suez Canal, and finally Dubai. Her arrival in Dubai on 26 November was met with great fanfare. Hundreds of small boats and pleasure craft met the ship as she rounded The World Islands. As she made her way to Port Rashid, an Emirates A380 flew overhead. *QE2* was later met by the Royal Yacht *Dubai* as well as the Royal Navy's HMS *Lancaster* – the latter honouring *QE2* with a traditional 'three cheers' salute.

As *QE2* berthed for the last time as an active Cunard liner, a light show and fireworks display illumined the night sky. With the smoke clearing and the ship alongside, passengers and crew were left to enjoy their final night aboard the world's best-loved ship.

fifteen

THE LONG SLEEP

It almost makes me think the *QE2* could work
here ... having evening drinks with this view.

Rob Lightbody, founder of The *QE2* Story forum,
while on Boat Deck in April 2011

On 27 November 2008, passengers awoke for their last morning aboard *QE2*. The mood from the night before had given way to the familiar yet surreal atmosphere of disembarkation. The flurry of activity to pack the final luggage items away, thank cabin attendants and indulge in a final breakfast was juxtaposed with the realisation that this was *QE2*'s last ever passenger disembarkation activity.

When the final passengers departed at around noon, the crew were left with their ship. Many of the crew had flights to catch over the next day, yet took the time to walk the decks and bid farewell to *QE2* in their own way. She had been their home away from home for years and in some cases decades.

That afternoon, a ceremony was held on the port Bridge wing. Here, a delegation from her new owners met with Cunard

Left and right: *QE2* as seen
from *QM2* alongside in 2009.
(Jan Frame)

The view of *QE2* from *QM2*'s foredeck in 2009. (Jan Frame)

QM2 met *QE2* in Port Rashid in 2009. (Jan Frame)

QE2 alongisde in Port Rashid as seen from the access road, 2009. (Jan Frame)

There are no more books in *QE2*'s bookshop. (Rob Lightbody)

QE2's priceless artwork collection was packaged up and stored in 2011. (Rob Lightbody)

officials for formal handover of the ship. Captain Ian McNaught made the final entry in *QE2*'s log, and the Cunard house flag was lowered and replaced with the flag of Nakheel. Around the world, thousands of *QE2* fans logged into the ship's live Bridge webcam to watch the lowering of the Cunard flag from the ship's bow. So many people across the world were on the website at the same time that load times were noticeably slow. *QE2* was a Cunard ship no more.

While she was retired from Cunard service, *QE2* remained a commissioned passenger ship. Commodore Ronald Warwick, who had commanded *QE2* from 1990 to 2003, had been appointed by Nakheel to command *QE2* once she arrived in Dubai. As such, he sailed with *QE2* on her final voyage and assumed command of the ship. This was to be a short-lived situation, as the published plans saw *QE2* due for a major refurbishment, after which she would be permanently berthed at the Palm Jumeirah as a floating hotel. However, the global financial crisis was having devastating economic effects around the world. Despite its wealth, Dubai was not immune, and after

several months it became evident that the *QE2* refurbishment was delayed. During this time, a small crew was employed to manage and maintain *QE2*. The ship remained alongside at the Port Rashid berth. Her engines were maintained, with each of the nine diesel generators cycled through to provide essential power and services to the ship. *QE2* looked ready to sail. She was painted and cleaned. Some of the areas of the ship that were showing signs of wear and tear were repaired by a passionate and dedicated team that adopted the ship as their own.

On several occasions between 2009 and 2012, *QE2* was joined in Dubai by Cunard's current Queens, with *QM2*, *Queen Victoria* and *Queen Elizabeth* all making calls to the port. In March 2009, just prior to *QM2*'s visit, the large Cunard lettering was removed from *QE2*'s hull. This was stored on the dockside.

Later in 2009, the ship was taken to the Dubai dry dock facility. It was widely speculated that she would sail for South Africa to be used as a floating hotel during the 2010 FIFA World Cup. The voyage to South Africa never materialised,

The *Mauretania* model in 2011. It formed part of *QE2*'s once impressive Heritage Trail. (Rob Lightbody)

Above: The Chartroom Bar has had its backlit panels removed and stored. (Rob Lightbody)

Right: Some artwork remains aboard, such as this portrait of HM the Queen Mother that once hung aboard RMS *Queen Elizabeth*. (Rob Lightbody)

and *QE2* was later moved to the inner harbour at Port Rashid. On 28 January 2011 the ship's mooring lines snapped during a sandstorm and she drifted into the harbour. Three tugs assisted the stricken liner and she was secured alongside once again.

Since 2009, Rob Lightbody and a team of dedicated *QE2* enthusiasts had been digitally cataloguing stories, events, timelines and memories from the ship's thirty-nine-and-a-half-year Cunard career. The digital repository takes the form of a web forum known as The *QE2* Story. In 2011, Rob Lightbody was invited aboard *QE2* to inspect and document the condition that the ship was in. He found a well-managed, much-loved liner with a passionate and dedicated crew now under the command of Captain William Cooper.

In the latter part of that year, news broke that *QE2* would host a lavish New Year's party. The first public event held aboard the ship since she arrived in Dubai, it included a 3D mapping visual show on the ship's superstructure, live music entertainment and cocktails served on the ship's aft decks.

Late the following year, *QE2*'s live-in crew departed the ship, which coincided with reports that the liner had been sold for scrap. In December a group called 'QE2 London' revealed their plans to return *QE2* to Great Britain to be opened as a floating hotel on the Thames, near the O2 Arena. However, these plans did not come to pass, with the ship instead moved to the Dubai dry dock. Prior to her relocation, it was revealed in a press conference that new plans existed to convert *QE2* into a floating hotel and relocate her to Asia. But the great liner remained at the dry dock for more than two years, with no internal refurbishment being completed. With her engines shut down and lighting extinguished, the internal cleanliness of the vessel deteriorated.

In August 2015 *QE2* was relocated from the dry dock back to Port Rashid. The dirty and forlorn liner was cleaned and given a fresh coat of paint. LED lighting was added to her Boat Deck level in October 2015, while string lighting was erected between her bow, mast, funnel and stern in December. In 2016 *QE2*'s lifeboats were lowered from Boat Deck. Those on the port side were lowered to the water while the starboard boats hovered above the dock. The boats were later removed and placed on the dockside. In August 2016 the lifeboat davits were cut off the ship – the first noticeable physical alteration made to the exterior of the vessel during her stay in Dubai.

As this book goes to print, *QE2* remains in cold lay-up. The ship that sailed more people further than any before her is ending the ninth year of her long sleep. *QE2* enthusiasts and the general public alike watch and wait to see what the future holds for the world's best-loved ship. It is the hope of many around the world that by the time you read these words a positive future for *QE2* has come to fruition.

AFTERWORD

BY COMMODORE JOHN BURTON-HALL

It is a great pleasure for me to write an Afterword for Chris and Rachelle's anniversary book on the most famous lady of the seas, as I served aboard her for over twenty-one years of my seagoing life. From when I was appointed her second officer, through my time as a hull surveyor during her last year of building on Clydebank, to when I had the privilege to become Cunard's first appointed commodore for many years (and *QE2*'s last), she became the other lady in my life.

I experienced most of her high points and, as has been written elsewhere, commanded her during her most trying and difficult times. The most beautiful and elegant ship that I ever encountered during my long career, she was a tribute to British shipbuilders of the time, sadly never to have been surpassed. The first ship of her class able to transit both the Suez and Panama Canals and built for the North Atlantic, her ability to cope with the most challenging weather conditions was unequalled. The affection and pride felt by all who sailed on her, ship's company and passengers, is unique, and was abundantly displayed on 11 November 2008, her last sailing, which, by an interesting concurrence, was Remembrance Day.

QE2's final voyage was marked by my wife, who invited HRH the Duke of Edinburgh to commemorate both occasions on board with us at a formal luncheon attended by the ship's surviving captains and those connected with her over the years. Afterwards we both stood on Quarter Deck with His Royal Highness, and Ian and Sue McNaught, as we were showered with a million poppies. This spectacle was followed by a Harrier Jump Jet dipping its nose three times in farewell to the lady.

Commodore John Burton-Hall on the Bridge of *QE2*. (Michael Gallagher / Cunard)

In my address to those assembled in the Queens Room, I said, 'No more will the VHF's circuits hear the call "Nab Pilot, Nab Pilot, this is *QE2*, Golf, Bravo, Tango, Tango."' GBTT was the great lady's signal letters, which she had inherited from the *Queen Mary*.

In this, her fiftieth year, let us raise a glass of wine to her, as it launched her on her way from the hand of her namesake, Queen Elizabeth II.

I regret that *QE2*, a unique piece of Britain's heritage, was not able to be kept on our shores. Failing this, I felt she should have been broken up, as was P&O's *Canberra* – an honourable end for a ship after a working life. I realise that this is difficult to comprehend for those not involved with the lives of ships, as indeed would be the concept of a ship having a persona. However, for those of us who are, I can assure you that many feel the former and most feel the latter. It is a supreme indignity to disembowel a glorious and heroic vessel and abandon her as a shell. It is, therefore, all the more necessary to reminisce, and to share with others not as privileged as we were, the eminence and nobility of this royal majesty of the seas. For it is in this that *QE2* is immortalised.

Port Bridge wing of the *QE2*. Commodore John Burton-Hall (*centre*) is bringing the ship alongside in the Port of Piraeus, assisted by First Officer Ian McNaught (*left*), now captain. (Rosie Burton-Hall)

BIBLIOGRAPHY

BOOKS

Baynard, F.O. and Miller, W.H. (1991) *Picture History of the Cunard Line, 1840–1990*, Dover Publications, United Kingdom.

Buchanan, G. (1996) *Queen Elizabeth 2: Sailing into the New Millennium*, Past and Present Publishing, United Kingdom.

Hutchings, D. (1990) *RMS Queen Elizabeth: From Victory to Valhalla*, Kingfisher Publications, United Kingdom.

Hutchings, D. (2002) *QE2: A Ship for all Seasons*, Waterfront, United Kingdom.

Miller, W.H. (1995) *Pictorial Encyclopedia of Ocean Liners, 1860 to 1994*, Constable and Company, United Kingdom.

Miller, W.H. (2001) *Picture History of British Ocean Liners, 1900 to Present*, Dover Publications, United Kingdom.

Peter, B., Dawson, P. and Johnston, I. (2008) *QE2: Britain's Greatest Liner*, Ferry Publications, United Kingdom.

Storey, T. (2007) *QE2: Farewell Queen of the Seas (40th Anniversary Tribute)*, Trinity Mirror Sport Media, United Kingdom.

Thatcher, C. (2007) *QE2: Forty Years Famous*, Simon & Schuster Ltd, United Kingdom.

Warwick, R.W. (1999) *QE2: The Cunard Line Flagship, Queen Elizabeth II*, third edition, Norton, United Kingdom.

Williams, D. (2004) *Cunard's Legendary Queens of the Seas*, Ian Allan Publishing, United Kingdom.

WEBSITES AND SOCIAL MEDIA

chrisframe.com.au – Chris Frame's maritime history website.
chriscunard.com – Chris & Rachelle's Cunard website.
theqe2story.com – The *QE2* Story website and forum.
qe2.org.uk – Sam Warwick's *QE2* website.
roblightbody.com – Rob Lightbody's website.
youtube.com @TheQE2Story - The *QE2* Story on Youtube.

NEWS ARTICLES

'*Queen Elizabeth* maiden voyage sells out faster than *QE2* farewell', from prnewswire.com, retrieved September 2016.

PERSONAL CORRESPONDENCE

Burton-Hall, Commodore J., *QE2* master.
Gallagher, Michael, Cunard historian.
Lightbody, Rob, The *QE2* Story forum.
McNaught, Captain I., *QE2* master.
Rynd, Commodore C., *QE2* master.
Warwick, Commodore R.W., *QE2* master.
Wells, Captain Chris, *QE2* master.
Yeoman, Chief Engineer P., *QE2* chief engineer.